CREDIT REPAIR SECRETS

2 Books in 1

Author : Frankie Brackett

DISCOVER THE MOST HIDDEN SECRETS FOR MANAGING YOUR CREDIT REPAIR & IMPROVE QUICKLY YOUR CREDIT SCORE & PERSONAL FINANCE TO ACHIEVE FINANCIAL FREEDOM AND ENJOY A NEW LIFESTYLE.

Table of Contents Book 1

Introduction 5

Chapter 1. How to Deal with Bankruptcy 7

Chapter 2. What Is Credit Repair and How Does It Work? 12

Chapter 3. Fair Credit Reporting Act Requirements 18

Chapter 4. What Is Section 609? 24

Chapter 5. Annual Credit Report 29

Chapter 6. Look for Errors in the Report 33

Chapter 7. Credit Scoring and the Automobile Industry 38

Chapter 8. Properly Dispute Negative Account 43

Chapter 9. The Truth About Credit Bureaus 50

Chapter 10. How Your Credit Repair Score Is Calculated 56

Chapter 11.	The Fico Credit Scores	61
Chapter 12.	Simple Steps to Fix Your Credit Scores	66
Chapter 13.	Is Credit Repair Ethical?	73
Chapter 14.	Why People and Companies Need Credit Repair	79
Chapter 15.	Effective Strategies for Repairing Your Credit	83
Chapter 16.	Credit Repair Services	88
Chapter 17.	Your Financial Freedom	91
Chapter 18.	Mindset	94
Conclusion		100

Table of Contents Book 2

Introduction		104
Chapter 1.	Most Important Things to Know About Credit Repair	105
Chapter 2.	Fair Credit Reporting Act	110
Chapter 3.	Section 609	115
Chapter 4.	The FICO Credit Scores	121
Chapter 5.	Look for Errors in the Report	127
Chapter 6.	Why People Need Credit Repair	130
Chapter 7.	What Is Credit Piggybacking	136
Chapter 8.	What the Lawyers Don't Want You to Know	140
Chapter 9.	How Credit Cards Effect Your Score	144
Chapter 10.	Debt-Snowball Method	150
Chapter 11.	How to Overcome Credit Card Debt?	153

Chapter 12. How to Fix Your Credit Yourself in 9 Easy Steps? 158

Chapter 13. How to Maintain It and Mindset 163

Chapter 14. How to Remove Extra Names and Addresses from Your Report? 169

Chapter 15. Delete Inquiries Like the Pros 174

Chapter 16. The FUQ'S (Frequently Unasked Questions): Things Everyone Should Know About Their Credit Score. 178

Chapter 17. How to Protect Your Credit and Credit Monitoring? 184

Chapter 18. Reach Your Financial Freedom 187

Chapter 19. Template Examples and Simulations 193

Conclusion 201

© **Copyright 2021 - All rights reserved.**

The content contained within this book may not be reproduced, duplicated or transmitted without direct written permission from the author or the publisher.

Under no circumstances will any blame or legal responsibility be held against the publisher, or author, for any damages, reparation, or monetary loss due to the information contained within this book. Either directly or indirectly.

Legal Notice:

This book is copyright protected. This book is only for personal use. You cannot amend, distribute, sell, use, quote or paraphrase any part, or the content within this book, without the consent of the author or publisher.

Disclaimer Notice:

Please note the information contained within this document is for educational and entertainment purposes only. All effort has been executed to present accurate, up to date, and reliable, complete information. No warranties of any kind are declared or implied. Readers acknowledge that the author is not engaging in the rendering of legal, financial, medical or professional advice. The content within this book has been derived from various sources. Please consult a licensed professional before attempting any techniques outlined in this book.

By reading this document, the reader agrees that under no circumstances is the author responsible for any losses, direct or indirect, which are incurred as a result of the use of information contained within this document, including, but not limited to, — errors, omissions, or inaccuracies.

Introduction Book 1

Credit repair can be very difficult. But by following the steps below, you'll find it's not as hard as you think. The best part is that there are really only three things that matter when it comes to credit repair: understanding your credit score, knowing what items to request for free removal from negative reports, and understanding how much time and money you would save with a cleaned-up credit report."

What exactly is credit repair? It's getting rid of negative information on your credit report that is preventing you from being able to take out loans or get new lines of credit. Some types of this negative information include not paying fees on time or having late payments made by collections agencies. If you have credit repair, you can stop paying late fees and start thinking about taking larger loans with good percentages.

If your credit is bad, it's important to understand how credit scoring works. There are three different explanations of how your credit score is calculated: Fair Isaac, FICO, and Vantage. These three scoring agencies also make up the three main companies that design credit scores. Most creditors will accept all three types of scores. A major factor in choosing a score to use is whether or not the creditor accepts reports from the three agencies. Being aware of which score is most accepted by financial institutions can make a big difference when applying for loans and other types of lines of credit.

Most people start their credit repair by getting negative items removed from their reports. Negative items include collections accounts and late payments made by collection agencies. You have to ask creditors what they charge for removing negative information from your credit report. For example, if they charge onetime fees per item removed, you can pay that amount and then ask them to remove all future negative items free-of-charge whenever you request it at that same time each year in the future. If they charge a yearly fee to remove negative items, you can just pay that amount in the beginning and then request full removal of all future negative items free-of-charge each year at that one time. A one-time charge is offered by some credit repair agencies, although this is not always the best option. Always check with creditors before doing this to make sure you qualify.

Credit repair can be very difficult if you don't understand how your credit score works and what needs to be removed from your credit report if you want new lines of credit. It is important to know what types of negative information are on your credit report and whether or not it's possible for them to remove it. The main thing to remember is that with regard to credit repair, only three things are important: knowing your credit score, knowing the items that need to be removed from negative reports for free, and knowing how much time and money you can save by saving money. Clean up credit reports.

Chapter 1. How to Deal with Bankruptcy

Whether you struggle with debt, are unable to meet all your payments on time, have missed multiple payments on your mortgage or car loan, have maxed out your credit cards, are balancing payments on a number of credit cards to try to keep up to date, or are slipping back on a lot of unsecured debt, the effective bankruptcy option may be what you need to offset your income and debt. If you think the worst possible thing for your credit is bankruptcy, think again. If you're already behind on payments and keep falling further behind or have accounts in collection, bankruptcy may help you start building a strong credit history sooner rather than later.

Before considering how bankruptcy will work for you, you must first familiarize yourself with the various types of bankruptcy, grasp what bankruptcy can and cannot do, and know how it will affect your reputation.

Bankruptcy is the kind of insolvency that most people have heard about. This helps you clear out most consumer debt: credit cards, medical bills, etc. However, in return, you may have to sell some of your properties, such as a second car, expensive electronic equipment, or a holiday home.

Filing for bankruptcy triggers a "complete hold" which automatically prevents most of your creditors from trying to collect what you owe them. Therefore, at least temporarily, creditors can't legally "garnish" (take) your wages; clear your bank account; go after your car, home, or other property; or shut off your services Before your bankruptcy case ends, your past financial issues are in the hands of the bankruptcy court.

A creditor may try to convince you to "reaffirm" (commit to pay off) a debt after your bankruptcy discharge before the insolvency process ends. Once you reassert a loan, think twice. You don't have to reaffirm that debt; if you do, you have to repay it even though all other loans have been paid back. Any arrangement with the bankruptcy court to reassert a loan must be written down and charged. Until the debts are forgiven or within 60 days after the settlement is deposited with the judge, you may void a reassertion deal. If a prosecutor hasn't helped you reach the reaffirmation deal, the court will accept it.

Bankruptcy is not for everybody; it goes without saying. An explanation is that some expenses cannot be washed out of bankruptcy, including:

- Child or spousal care commitments
- Student loans, unless reimbursement will bring you undue hardship (which is very difficult to prove)
- Court-ordered restitution— payments you are ordered to make after a criminal conviction
- Some federal, state, and municipal income taxes longer than three years past due, and any money due.
- Debt on account of death or injury incurred by the intoxicated driving
- Debt on behalf of a marriage settlement agreement or divorce order
- Debt you fail to mention in your bankruptcy documents, unless the claimant hears about your bankruptcy throughout due time.
- Debts the bankruptcy judge regulates were incurred as a result of misconduct on your part — for example, debts incurred as a result of deception (such as lying on a credit application or writing a bad check), malicious harm (such as assault, battery, false imprisonment, libel, or slander), larceny (theft), or breach of confidence or embezzlement.

Not everyone can make use of bankruptcy. Here are some situations when you will not qualify:

- In this case, you earned discharge of your creditors after eight years of filing your new lawsuit (unless you paid 100% of your previously unsecured debts).
- You received debt relief in the case you filed within six years of filing your current 7 cases.
- You have defrauded creditors.

- An earlier bankruptcy lawsuit you brought has been dismissed within the last 180 days because you violated a court order, failed to appear in court as necessary, the court found that your filing was false or represented a misuse of the bankruptcy procedure, or you demanded dismissal after a creditor asked the court to lift the automatic stay.
- The estimated income for a family of your size in the six months before you register is higher than the average income in your state, and you would have enough money left to pay your loans over a five-year term after subtracting all approved expenses. This requirement is referred to as "the test of means," and those who do not pass it may be required to use bankruptcy.

If you have a steady income and think you could squeeze out regular monthly payments. Allows you to keep your property and use your disposable income to pay all or a portion of your debts over three to five years.

You normally have to pay 100 percent of the child support due, for example, but you probably wouldn't have to pay off your credit card debts entirely. To make the bills you can use salaries, bonuses, investment income, business income, or any other money.

Many people file for bankruptcy because they can set up a recovery plan to bring in the new unpaid mortgage or car payments and get back on track for their original loan, to pay off a tax debt without the possibility of foreclosure or repossession.

Nonetheless, these are not the only reasons people file for bankruptcy.

If you cannot fulfill a repayment plan—for example, you lose your job in the scheme for six months and can't make the payments— the bankruptcy court will have the authority to change the program. If the situation seems acute, a grace period, an extended repayment period or a decrease of the total amount due may be offered. If it is clear that due to circumstances beyond your control, you cannot actually fulfill the agreement, the bankruptcy court may even authorize you to discharge (cancel) your debts on the grounds of hardship.

If the bankruptcy court does not authorize you to change your agreement or award you discharge for disability, you have the right to:

- Convert to a bankruptcy
- Dismiss your case if the bankruptcy court won't let you modify your plan or give you a discharge of hardships. A dismissal of your lawsuit will leave you in the same place as before you sued because you owe less due to the contributions you made. The benefit that was withheld from the time you filed the claim until it was rejected will be added to the debt by your creditors.

Bankruptcy and Credit Repair: Does It Help or Hurt?

Bankruptcy is a powerful tool for removing or rising most unsecured debts, and can even cut down on most secured debts— giving you a fresh start. But it will live up to 10 years on your credit report (longer if you apply for a $150,000 or more loan), which is longer than almost any other derogatory thing in your history.

Even though a bankruptcy will lower your credit score immediately, the impact may be smaller than you think.

"Someone who had spotless credit and a very good FICO score might expect a huge decrease in their ratings, according to Fair Isaac.

On the other hand, someone with more derogatory things already reported on their credit report could only see a small decrease in their ratings. "Fair Isaac also warns that the greater the effect on your ranking, the more accounts included in the bankruptcy filing. Doesn't make much of a difference, however— according to Fair Isaac, both have an equally negative effect on your credit score.

Ironically, a bankruptcy will help you start building good credit faster than if you don't file for bankruptcy and keep struggling with more debt than you can afford, particularly if you end up filing bankruptcy again later. Eliminating or eliminating loans by bankruptcy would help you (when the bankruptcy is over) accomplish the two most important goals for a good credit score: meeting your payments on time (35% of your FICO score) and not using the bulk of your available credit (30% of your FICO score). Creditors differ in the way they can offer credit or good interest rates and repayment conditions shortly after a bankruptcy, but they tend to treat the most recent credit issues as more relevant than older problems.

Getting a Mortgage after Bankruptcy

Following one year of interest in a repayment plan, the Federal Housing Administration (FHA) must cover lenders, for two years following discharge. It will consider insuring lenders even more easily following foreclosure, in extenuating circumstances. The FHA needs you to make payments on time and that your interest balances are correct or you don't have new credit commitments after a bankruptcy.

Fannie Mae will not purchase homes if a discharge happened less than two years prior, or a discharge occurred less than four years prior. Private lenders not offering their loans to Fannie Mae may be subject to stricter requirements.

Getting a Credit Card

For many creditors, your sharply reduced debts after bankruptcy and the several-year ban on filing bankruptcy again make you an attractive candidate for credit card offers.

In the past, individuals who filed for bankruptcy, shortly after receiving their bankruptcy discharge, reported receiving several credit cards bids. Banks pulled back on credit card offers during the crisis, but by late 2010, banks were again providing credit cards to people without good credit. Chances are after a foreclosure you'll be able to get credit cards soon. Nonetheless, keep in mind that these cards are expected to carry high-interest rates, annual fees, and other heavy costs.

Chapter 2. What Is Credit Repair and How Does It Work?

Does credit fix truly work? It's an inquiry that has been posed on many occasions by shoppers whose credit score has run into some bad luck and who are prepared to get their budgetary life in the groove again.

Albeit not many of us truly appreciate ads intruding on our favored programming, a large number of us are still surprisingly ready to appreciate an item promotion when it's the superstar — thus, the infomercial. Maybe it's the puzzle, all things considered, since, as a rule, we're left contemplating the item and attempting to choose, "Accomplishes it truly work?!"

Like the mop that vows to clean anything, credit fix can often appear just as it couldn't in any way, shape, or form be the credit report enchantment eraser it's often promoted to be. In any case, hearing the narratives, perusing the surveys, and paging through gathering posts can show blended outcomes, leaving you with that equivalent essential inquiry: "Credits fix truly work?!" In the accompanying book, we'll answer this significant question and give important data on the most proficient method to get your credit score back to a decent number.

Indeed, So Long as Your Items Qualify for Dispute

With everything taken into account, the response to the subject of whether credit fix works is a lot of a run of the mill, "Truly, however... "Yes, credit fix can work to expel certain negative things from your credit reports. Be that as it may, it doesn't work for each kind of thing — and it unquestionably isn't a prompt, enchantment credit score sponsor.

Basically, credit fix is the way toward questioning things on your credit report that are an out-of-line or wrong portrayal of your monetary history. The capacity to record credit report questions is given to assist you with guaranteeing your credit report isn't brimming with bogus information that can be utilized against you in loaning choices.

If you identify data in your document that is deficient or mistaken, and report it to the purchaser detailing the organization, the office must research except if your debate is trivial. — FTC

What credit fix isn't is a simple method to expel genuinely earned critical credit report marks or an approach to discard real obligations. Not exclusively are these debates liable to be dismissed, yet the credit departments don't have to research questions that are viewed as negligible.

The Most Likely to Be Successfully Disputed Items

The most ideal approach to have credit fix achievement is to realize what's in store from the procedure before you begin. If you go into it with an expanded feeling of what you'll achieve, you'll clearly be baffled at long last. Reasonable desires can go far in credit fix (and money when all is said in done).

Along these lines, it boils down to knowing which things on your credit report really meet the qualifications for a fruitful debate.

Since the procedure is intended to guarantee your reports are exact, the sorts of things that can ordinarily be expelled through credit fix are those that are, well, off base here and there. This incorporates things that are wrong, false, obsolete, or unverified.

Mistaken Items

The least demanding kind of thing to contest is one that is only completely incorrect. This spreads fundamental blunders, such as spelling botches or distorted sums that can create turmoil or credit issues. For instance, if that decimal point is in an inappropriate spot, it might seem as though you have unquestionably more obligation than you should. Much of the time, basic slip-ups require little exertion for the credit department to explore and can be fixed in a genuinely short measure of time.

Obsolete Items

Another sort of questionable thing that is commonly simple to fix are things that are obsolete. Most negative things can just stay on your credit report for a set measure of time before they should be expelled. Hard credit requests, for example, last as long as two years, while reprobate installments can last up to seven. When these things hit their maximum age, be that as it may, they ought to be expelled from your report consequently or you can record a debate to have them evacuated.

Fake Items

If you've at any point been the survivor of data fraud, you could end up with fake records on your credit reports. While these records may appear to be authentic from the outset, further examination can often disclose their vile birthplaces. Notwithstanding documenting debates to have fake records expelled from your reports, make certain to report any instances of fraud immediately.

Unconfirmed Items

The remainder of the as often as possible contested things are those records on your reports that can't be validated by the data suppliers. If they can't show that the obligation or deprecatory imprint truly has a place with you, the credit departments will evacuate the thing.

When considering a credit fix, make certain to check each of the three of your credit reports. Credit authorities depend on outsiders to report your money-related conduct, so few out of every odd thing is accounted for to each of the three buyer credit departments (Equifax, Experian, and TransUnion).

Thus, a couple of your credit reports could house questionable things that don't appear on different reports. Since you can't foresee which credit report(s) a creditor will use to decide your credit hazard, every one of the three of your reports ought to be in acceptable condition to forestall passing up credit later on.

The Top Credit Repair Companies

Similarly, as with numerous things in life, credit fix is a procedure that you can do yourself — or you can recruit an expert. The course you take will rely for the most part upon you (and your credit reports). If your credit report questions are basic and clear, for example, a spelling mistake or obsolete thing, then documenting yourself might be quick and simple.

If your questions are increasingly included, in any case, it might be less upsetting to employ an accomplished credit fix organization to follow up for your benefit. This can be especially obvious in situations where you have to introduce significant proof to back up your debate. A portion of our top-of-the-line credit fix organizations has many years of experience helping purchasers expel things from their credit reports.

Most credit fix organizations will work under a month-to-month expense, which is charged for every month that they chip away at your sake. Credit fix is once in a while a brisk procedure, so be set up to pay for the administration for at any rate a couple of months if you go that course. Convoluted credit fix cases including different debates may take a half year or more to get results.

One thing to note is that credit fix organizations can't lawfully ensure positive outcomes (at any rate, not in such a significant number of words). If a credit correction organization guarantees that you will see a specific number of things thrown out of their reports, you may need to take a closer look at the organization's visibility, or just make another decision.

How the Credit Repair Process Works

Contesting wrong things on your credit report is a legitimate right allowed to you by the Fair Credit Reporting Act (FCRA), which secures your entitlement to reasonable and precise credit reports.

While debates once should have been submitted recorded as a hard copy through the mail, even the credit authorities have modernized to where you can document most questions online through the department's site. By all accounts, credit fix seems like a straightforward procedure. What's more, it very well maybe. "Be that as it may, " The multifaceted nature of the procedure will in general change with the idea of your debates.

To begin, a different question should be petitioned for everything and for each credit report. This implies you'll require three individual debates to evacuate a solitary thing that shows up on every one of the three reports, which should be finished by composing letters to every department or visiting every authority's site.

When you present your debate, you should make certain to incorporate the same number of supporting or potentially evidentiary reports as you can. Continuously submit duplicates with your question, never present your unique reports.

You'll additionally need to keep a duplicate of your contest and any correspondence identified with it — just on the off chance that an issue emerges.

When a contest is gotten by the agency, it has 30 days to examine the thing being referred to and react to your debate. Some portion of this prerequisite is that the organization should advance your debate and any data you give to the gathering that gave the data.

The data supplier should then explore the thing being referred to, looking into all applicable data and announcing the outcomes to the credit agency. If the data furnisher sees the thing as off base, it is required to notify every one of the three credit departments and solicitation that the thing be expelled from the entirety of your credit reports.

After the examination, the authority is required to illuminate you regarding the outcomes recorded as a hard copy, alongside a duplicate of your report if things were adjusted. You can likewise demand the announcing organization to send notification of these amendments to any individual who has gotten your credit report in the previous half-year.

Fix the Root of Your Credit Problems for Lasting Success

While the late-night infomercial might be as much about the promoting as the "stunning" items it highlights, it unquestionably doesn't lessen the feeling of the puzzle that originates from thinking about whether that little device truly is the wonder they portray it. Be that as it may, even apparently innocuous infomercials can turn grievous for the individuals who genuinely need whatever contraption they're selling to really work.

For some, shoppers, a credit fix can from the start appear to be a simple method to clean away the credit harm holding down their credit scores. Shockingly, credit fix is one item that doesn't "do everything" — paying little heed to how it's occasionally publicized.

While this shouldn't imply that credit fix doesn't work — it does, give your contested things meet the necessities — however, it positively isn't a fix-all. The most ideal approach to guarantee enduring credit achievement is to address the issues that made you search out credit fix in any case.

Chapter 3. Fair Credit Reporting Act Requirements

The federal law governing credit reporting is the Fair Credit Reporting Act (FCRA).

Congress enacted the FCRA in 1970 to give consumers more control over what information goes into their credit history.

The FCRA sets limits on who can access consumer credit reports, how their information is used, and how long it stays on file. It also provides for an avenue of recourse if a person believes that inaccurate information has been reported.

If you have questions about the requirements of the FCRA or need assistance with any aspect thereof, please contact our experienced attorneys for a consultation.

Legislative History

The Fair Credit Reporting Act (FCRA), Pub. L. No. 90-321, 82 Stat. 168 (1966), codified at 15 U.S.C. § 1681 et seq., was enacted by Congress on October 27, 1970, in response to government surveys which revealed widespread inaccurate information reported by consumer reporting agencies about the personal histories of consumers. The Act "was designed to revise the practices of such agencies by limiting their access to certain records" and "to review the accuracy of their reports." Although it is not a criminal statute, it significantly changed the practices of many federal and state agencies that previously had access to credit reports without limits.

The Act is codified at 15 U.S.C. § 1681-1681q, and became effective on October 20, 1971. Among other things, the FCRA requires consumer reporting agencies to maintain reasonable procedures for verifying the accuracy of the information concerning consumers that they furnish to third parties and establishes procedures under which consumers may dispute the accuracy of such information.

The FCRA confers broad powers upon both federal and state regulatory agencies. The Act establishes a Federal Trade Commission (FTC) Bureau of Consumer Protection to administer and enforce its provisions directly or through delegation to other appropriate federal or state agencies. Each agency designated by the FTC has primary enforcement responsibility with respect to particular types of entities. For example, the FTC designates the Federal Reserve Board as the agency responsible for administering and enforcing the Act's requirements regarding consumer reports that are used or disseminated by banks.

The Act authorizes other federal agencies to enforce compliance with its requirements. The U.S. Postal Service, for example, is authorized by 15 U.S.C. § 1681s-2 to enforce compliance with certain requirements of the FCRA with respect to consumer reports relating to credit transactions involving the mail. The Federal Trade Commission, in turn, shares enforcement authority over the same provisions with state attorneys general under 15 U.S.C. § 1681s-6.

The FCRA also imposes certain conditions on certain types of business entities. For example, an insurance company must comply with the FCRA if it furnishes a consumer report to a person who is seeking to obtain credit. It also imposes requirements on banks with respect to deposit holding companies and their affiliates.

Personal Information

Certain kinds of personal information are excluded from the Act's scope. It does not apply to information regarding tenancies of real estate that is used for no purpose other than to enable the owner to collect the rent or to protect the premises. The Act's requirements do not apply to information relating to securities or commodities transactions, nor does it cover any "consumer report [that] contains any ... credit score or any other risk score or predictability indicator

There are two exceptions to the prohibition against obtaining credit reports without prior written notice. The Fair Credit Reporting Act does not apply to "the communication of a credit report by any person to whom such report is communicated in accordance with the standardized Mortgage Data Bank System of Department of Housing and Urban development. "Also, the FCRA does not apply when a person "furnishes information to a consumer reporting agency regarding any inquiry made by such person for use in determining the propriety of granting credit to an individual."

Consumer Reports

Any written, oral, or other contact by a consumer reporting agency that provides information about a consumer's creditworthiness, credit status, or creditworthiness is called a consumer report (also known as a background check). This includes a consumer's credit history and any information that is compiled using any of the information in a credit report.

Consumer Reporting Agencies

A consumer reporting agency (CRA) is defined as any person who regularly engages in assembling or evaluating consumer credit information or other information on consumers for the purpose of furnishing consumer reports to third parties. The definition specifically excludes persons who assemble or evaluate consumer credit information only for the purposes of "applications for, or operation of, a person's business by which loans are originated" and "debt collecting activities under [the Fair Debt Collection Practices Act] ... [and] insurance activities... in connection with insurance issued by persons other than such creditors.

Consumer reporting agencies are subject to a number of requirements contained in the Fair Credit Reporting Act. Among them is a requirement to regularly review their files on consumers to identify information that is inaccurate, obsolete, or of insufficient importance to warrant keeping, and remove that information. The information must be removed when it is more than seven years old in the case of adverse actions and more than six months old for bankruptcy filings. The FCRA also requires consumer reporting agencies to keep, for at least five years, written records regarding consumer complaints received by them.

Consumer reports may be obtained by employers during the pre-employment process. It does not require an employer to obtain a consumer report on an individual it is considering hiring, however; additional requirements may apply in that situation.

The FCRA's obligations apply only to consumer reporting agencies that "regularly" provide credit reports. This is defined as at least one credit report per month for each consumer whose credit information is in their files, and at least 20 or more such reports in any year. A single "credit report" may be composed of various information from different sources; for example, a single report might summarize all the information contained in three credit reports. The FCRA sets up a national system of self-regulation for consumer reporting agencies. Consumer reporting agencies are subject to periodic examination by the Federal Trade Commission (FTC) and must meet minimum standards that are set up by the FTC. Consumer reporting agencies may not charge consumers fees for placing, removing, or correcting information in their reports; however, a consumer reporting agency may charge its regular and reasonable fees to describe its services and any additional information it provides upon request. The maximum amount that a consumer reporting agency may charge for providing copies of records is $12.50 per consumer report. There are additional rules governing the sale of information obtained from a credit report in connection with the sale of goods or services.

Consumer reporting agencies have been under scrutiny and criticism lately for their business practices, as they have become powerful corporations and an increasingly important part of the economy. The changing economic market has meant that consumer reports are getting more detailed and complicated, but federal guidelines mean that only so much information can be included in any given credit report. The issue remains that, despite these legally imposed restrictions, a credit report may contain information that is not accurate, and there have been instances of identity theft as a result. Also, because the existing federal regulations are not made binding on states with respect to consumer reporting agencies located in their jurisdictions, major state governments have had to enact similar laws governing consumer reporting agencies.

The Fair Credit Reporting Act (FCRA) is enforced by the Federal Trade Commission (FTC). The FTC has an established complaint procedure for consumers and businesses affected by credit reports. Additionally, the FTC or private citizens also can bring lawsuits against credit bureaus that wrongfully deny consumers access to their reports or fail to correct errors in their reports.

History

The Federal Trade Commission (FTC) began examining the use of credit information in consumer reports as early as the 1950s. In 1973, the FTC held the first public hearings on pre-employment credit checks, and in 1974, the Commission held hearings about unfair and deceptive practices in the sale of credit reports. In 1977, Congress authorized federal agencies to investigate "unfair or deceptive acts or practices" by consumer reporting agencies. The FCRA was enacted in response to these investigations.

The Act establishes a Bureau of Consumer Protection within the Federal Trade Commission (FTC) to administer and enforce its provisions. The Bureau is required to perform investigations and audits and to issue reports of its activities. The FTC also has the power to bring civil actions to enforce compliance with the Act, as well as the ability to obtain injunctions and assess civil penalties.

Credit reporting agencies are subject to a number of requirements contained in the FCRA. Among them is a requirement that they regularly review their files on consumers to identify information that may be inaccurate, obsolete, or of insufficient importance or value to warrant keeping. Credit reporting agencies must make reasonable efforts to notify consumers when information is removed from a consumer report because it does not meet the criteria for inclusion. In addition, agencies must maintain a toll-free telephone number to allow consumers to get additional information about their reports, and to challenge information that they believe is inaccurate. They also must not charge consumers fees for placing, removing, or correcting information in the consumer's report.

Credit reporting agencies are prohibited from taking adverse action against any consumer because of any inquiry concerning a consumer's creditworthiness, credit standing, or credit capacity that was made by or on behalf of the consumer. Credit reporting agencies must make a consumer report available to anyone who is authorized to obtain the consumer report. They may not sell or rent information about consumers to a third party unless the information is aggregated or de-identified.

Credit bureaus and "consumer reporting agencies" are prohibited from including any derogatory information about an individual in a consumer report if they know the information is false, or if they have reasonable grounds to believe it is false. The Federal Trade Commission has published detailed guidelines as well as fact sheets on its website explaining how these rules apply in specific situations. For example, the FTC states that a "credit check typically includes information from various sources. The credit report includes information from the consumer's credit history and financial obligations. Information about the consumer's employment, assets, debts, income and taxes is obtained by contacting the employer of the consumer and other individuals who know about the consumer."

Consumer reporting agencies must provide consumers with some types of free reports for up to three years. They also must make certain disclosures regarding their policies for providing reports to third parties. For example, they must let consumers know if they are restricting access to their reports or if they will be sharing information with a third party (including employers or insurance companies) without obtaining advance consent. The agency also must provide consumers with information about whether the agency uses a consumer's credit report as part of its decision-making process, and explain how the agency obtains and uses this information.

Congress set up some rules for how consumer reporting agencies operate that apply only to those agencies located in different states from the state where the consumer lives. For example, if a consumer lives in New York but his or her credit report is maintained by a company based in Florida, that company must comply with New York state laws.

Chapter 4. What Is Section 609?

A 609 is known as a dispute letter, which you would send to your creditor if you saw you were overcharged or unfairly charged. Most people use a 609 letter in order to get the information they feel they should have received. There are several reasons why some information might be kept from you.

A section 609 letter is sent after two main steps. First, you see that the dispute is on your credit report. Second, you have already filed and processed a debt validation letter. The basis of the letter is that you will use it in order to take unfair charges off your credit report, which will then increase your credit score.

The 609 letters can easily help you delete your bad credit. Other than this, there are a couple of other benefits you will receive from the letter. One of these benefits is that you will obtain your documentation and information as the credit bureau has to release this information to you. Secondly, you will be able to obtain an accurate credit report, which can definitely help you increase your credit score.

There are also disadvantages to the 609 letters. One of these disadvantages is that collection agencies can add information to your credit history at any time. A second disadvantage is that you still have to repay debt. You cannot use the 609 letters in order to remove the debt that you are obligated to pay. Finally, your creditor can do their investigation and add the information back into your credit report, even if it was removed (Irby, 2019).

One of the reasons section 609 came to be is because one of five people state they have inaccurate information on the credit report (Black, 2019). At the same time, many people believe that this statistic is actually higher than 20 percent of Americans.

How Section 609 Works to Repair Bad Credit

If you notice anything on your report that should not be there, you need to use the section 609 loophole in order to file a dispute, which could result in their wrong information being taken off of the report. If this is the case, your credit score will increase, as you will no longer have this negative inaccuracy affecting your score.

How to File a Dispute with Section 609

It is important to note that there are several template letters for section 609. This means you can quickly and easily download and use one of these models. While you usually have to pay for them, there are some for free. Of course, you must remember to include your information in the letter before you send it.

You should make sure all the procedure is done correctly, as this will make it more likely that the information will come off and no one will place it back on your report again.

1. Find a dispute letter through googling "section 609 dispute letters." While you might be able to find a free download, for some, you will be able to copy and paste into Microsoft Word or onto a Google Doc.
2. Make the necessary changes to the letter. This will include changing the name and address. You must also make sure your phone number is included. Sometimes people include the email address, but this is not necessary. In fact, it is always safer to only include your home address or PO Box information. You must also check the whole letter. If something does not match what you want to say, such as what you are trying to dispute on your credit report, you need to state this. These letters are quite generic, which means you need to add in your information.
3. Make sure that all of the account information you want to be taken off your credit report is handwritten. Likewise, we recommend you use blue ink rather than black. On top of this, you do not need to worry about being too neat, but make sure they can read the letters and numbers correctly. This is an important part of filing your dispute letter because handwritten ones in blue ink will not be pushed through their automated system. They have an automatic system that will read the letter for them and punch in the account number you use. They will then send you a generic letter that states these accounts are now off your credit report, which does not mean that it

actually happened. When you write the information down, a person needs to read it and will typically take care of it. Of course, there's always the chance that you'll be ignored. Unfortunately, this can happen with any letters.

4. You must prove who you are with your letters. While this is never a comfortable thing to do, you must send a copy of your social security card and your driver's license or they will shred your letter. You also need to make sure that you get each of your letters notarized. You will usually do this by going to the courthouse in your district.

5. You can send as many letters as you need; however, keep in mind that the creditor typically will not make you send more than four. This is because when you threaten to take them to court in the third letter, they will realize that your accounts and demands just are not worth it. First, you could damage their reputation, and secondly, you will cost them more money than simply taking the information off your credit report will.

6. It is necessary to keep all correspondence they send you. When they try to force you to submit more information or keep telling you that they can't do something, this will come in handy. It is important that you do not surrender. Many people struggle to get them to pay attention because that is just how the system works. Therefore, you should not listen to their quick automatic reply that your information is off your credit report. You should also wait at least three months and then re-run your credit report to make sure the wrong information has been removed. Keep track of every time you need to re-run your credit report as you can use this as proof if they continue to send you a letter stating the information is off of your credit report.

It is important to note that you can now file a dispute letter online with all three credit bureaus. However, this is a new system, which means that it does come with more problems than sending one through the mail. While it is completely your choice whether you use a form to file your 609 dispute or send a letter, you should always keep copies and continue to track them, even if you don't hear from the credit bureau after a couple of months. It will never hurt to send them a second letter or even a third.

What Are My Rights Under 609?

The Fair Credit Reporting Act is going to cover many of the aspects and the components of credit checking to make sure that it is able to maintain a reasonable amount of privacy and accuracy along the way. This agency is going to list all of the responsibilities that credit reporting companies and any credit bureaus will have, and it includes the rights of the consumer that will be your rights in this situation. This Act is going to be the part that will govern how everything is going to work to ensure that all parties are treated in a fair manner.

When using this act, the consumer has to be told if any of the information on your file has been in the past or is now being used against you in any way, shape, or form. You have a right to know whether the information is harming you and what that information is.

In addition, the consumer is going to have the right to go through and dispute any information that may be seen as inaccurate or incomplete at the time. If they see that there are items in the documents they are sent, if the billing to them is not right or there is something else off in the process, the consumer has the right to dispute this and the credit reporting agency needs to at least look into it and determine if the consumer is right.

This Act is going to limit the access that third parties can have to your file. You personally have to go through and provide your consent before someone is able to go through and look at your credit score, whether it is a potential employer or another institution providing you with funding.

They are not able to get in and just look at it. Keep in mind that if you do not agree for them to take a look at the information, it is going to likely result in you not getting the funding that you want, because there are very few ways that the institution can fairly assess the risk that you pose to them in terms of creditworthiness.

It means that you may have debt or another negative item on your credit report, but there is a way to get around this without having to wait for years to get that to drop off your report or having to pay back a debt that you are not able to afford.

Keep in mind that this is not meant to be a method for you to take on many debts that you cannot afford and then just dump them. But on occasion, there could be a few that you are able to fight and get an instant boost to your credit score in the process.

Why Use a 609 Letter?

The 609 Letter is going to be one of the newest credit repair secrets that will help you remove a lot of information on your credit report, all of the false information, and sometimes even the accurate information, thanks to a little loophole found in our credit reporting laws. You can use this kind of letter in order to resolve some of the inaccuracies that show up, to dispute your errors, and handle some of the other items that could inaccurately come in and impact and lower your credit score.

Using these 609 letters is a good way for us to clean up our credit a bit and in some cases, it is going to make a perfect situation. However, we have to remember that outside of some of the obvious benefits that we are going to discuss, there are a few things that we need to be aware of ahead of time.

There are few limitations that are going to come with this as well. For example, even after you work with the 609 letters, it is possible that any information considered as accurate could be added to the report again, even after the removal. This is going to happen if the creditor is able to verify the accuracy. They may take it off for a bit if the 30 days have passed and they are not able to verify at that point. But if the information is accurate, remember that it could end up back on the report.

Chapter 5. Annual Credit Report

An annual credit report is a free service that lets you see what details credit reporting agencies to have on you. This is a valuable thing to do every year to make sure your report is accurate and up-to-date.

Discovering inaccuracies on your credit report can be difficult, as it may not be easy or possible for you to find them on your own. There are many companies that offer this service for a fee but it's best to check with the agencies first before paying someone else because they may charge more than necessary or provide less information than they would otherwise if you contacted them directly.

In some cases, the company will offer services similar in function as those offered by AnnualCreditReport.com, which does not itself release any credit report information to the public. The company may also ask you to sign an agreement that states you won't release the information to anyone else, but these agreements are often reversed by court order and are therefore unenforceable.

Annual Credit Report: What You Need to Know

Nobody wants a low credit score. That said, there are a lot of things that people don't know about their credit report and how it affects their scores more than they realize. One of those crucial tidbits that most people don't know is that they can purchase an annual credit report and see for themselves what is going on with their own personal finances.

Understanding the Annual Credit Report

The truth is that most people have no idea what an annual credit report is, and some may think it's a scam. It is not a scam, although there are some who will try to make a quick buck by offering you something that has no real value for you. But if you understand the basics of your credit report and what truly goes into it, then you will be more likely to realize when something you get in the mail from an unknown source is not worth your time or money.

Did You Know? People can purchase their own credit reports once every 12 months for free. Federal law mandates that everyone's credit report be available to them on request, and this is what an annual credit report is. The free report is expected to contain all of the specifics of your personal credit history from Equifax, Experian, and TransUnion, the three main credit bureaus.

What Does an Annual Credit Report Contain?

The annual credit report includes everything that is in your current credit report including:

- When was the last time you demanded to see a sample of your own work?
- The length of time each account has been open and how long it's been since you have updated any information on it.
- The accounts that you have listed as public records
- The accounts that you have listed as paid collections.
- What goes on with the accounts you have listed as bad credit loans.

There are other details of your credit report that will be included in your annual credit report, and it is up to you to thoroughly look over the information and make sure it's an accurate representation of what is in your credit report. If there are mistakes, then you must contact the appropriate agency or company immediately so they can fix the problem. Although it might not seem to be a major issue, even a minor mistake on your credit report can cause problems when applying for a loan. Some credit reporting agencies are not required to fix mistakes, so you could find yourself having to pay for a service you do not need.

Why It's Important for You to Know about Your Credit Report

A good credit score is a key ingredient in people who want to access loans, and it may seem like the best way to get a good credit score is to just keep on paying off debt until there isn't any left at all. This is an excellent example of how money can lead to problems, and you can avoid falling into the same pit.

You should check your credit report to see how much of your debt is due to loans. For example, if you're carrying a balance on just one or two credit cards, then it can be very easy to pay them off. The problem is that those balances will remain in your report and not appear to you as paid off. There are other accounts that can accumulate over time, like medical bills or even public record debts like tax liens. It's best to research the good and bad in every account before you go into debt if you want to have a better understanding of what's on your credit report and know what problems could arise down the road if there are mistakes in your report.

Getting a free copy of your credit report might seem like a waste of time, but you will be able to get an accurate sense of what's on your report and how it's affecting your current credit rating. It's also a good idea to double-check that anything in your current report is right, so you can contact the appropriate agencies if anything is missing or wrong.

What Is the Best Way to Get a Copy of Your Credit Report?

The process for getting a copy of your own credit report varies from state to state and can be different in other countries as well. You can find some great tips for how to get access to your own credit report here. But in a nutshell, it's as simple as going to the credit bureau website and requesting a copy of your credit report.

The site will tell you where to send the information or you can go ahead and email them directly. If you're feeling a little overwhelmed, then send everything at once and make sure to check everything for accuracy. If anything is in error, then you should contact the appropriate company immediately so they can look into it.

What Is an Annual Credit Report Worth?

The obvious question is: does an annual credit report have any real value? The answer in most cases is no, and this is because you do not need to see your own annual report every year. In fact, it might be better to wait a few years until you really need to access your report and look at the information. By then you can get a clearer picture of your credit history and see if there are any errors in your report or if there is anything you can do to fix them.

It's important to realize that more than likely you will not have any new debt or credit cards added to your report, so there is little reason for you to get a copy every year. The only time you should request an annual credit report is if something doesn't seem quite right about the information in your current report. If you get a bad score, then you want to investigate the reason why. It could be that there is some inaccurate information on your report or someone else's report with your same name listed as a previous address. If you have ever been involved in identity theft before, then this may be an important step in keeping your personal information safe and secure. Anytime you look at your credit report, make sure that the company is giving you a free copy and not charging for it.

Other good ways to find out how good your credit is and what problems you might face in the future are available as well. You will find more information on that topic in our guide. In short, you'll want to make sure your credit score is as good as possible if you want to take advantage of the many great offers available and maintain financial power.

Chapter 6.   Look for Errors in the Report

You need to eliminate all harmful credit report errors and inaccuracies from all three credit bureaus. The U.S. Public Interest Research Group (PIRG), an advocacy group, released a survey indicating that seven out of every ten credit reports contained some kind of error or mistake. The survey also found one out of every four credit reports had errors considered serious enough to prevent a borrower from getting a loan or credit. This survey shows we need to actively make sure our credit report is accurate. You are working hard to build your credit, do not allow other people's errors to negatively affect you...To hinder your hard work and earned rewards.

Every credit report is built on information gathered, purchased, and/or reported by creditors and third-party groups. If false or inaccurate information has made it to your credit report, then your credit report will reflect this false or inaccurate information. False or inaccurate information on your credit report can damage your credit, and cause you to pay higher interest rates, credit fees, and loan costs, or even prevent you from obtaining loans.

The sooner you identify harmful errors or inaccuracies in your credit report and work with your creditor and credit bureau to correct them, the sooner your credit score will improve. However, not all errors and inaccuracies are harmful.

1. Credit scenario: a revolving credit account (such as a credit card) was opened over 12 months ago, the credit limit is $1,000.00, the balance owed is three hundred dollars or less, and all monthly payments have been made on time.
2. Not harmful: any increase to your credit history or your credit limit only helps your credit and should not be corrected.
3. Harmful: any decrease made to your credit history, either to your credit limit or the report of any late payments, is harmful and should be corrected as soon as possible.

- Credit experts recommend individuals review their credit reports at least once every 12 months for harmful inaccuracies and errors. Data on how to order free credit reports are found below.
- It is important to verify the accuracy of dates, especially on every negative credit report. Bankruptcy, foreclosures, repossessions, late payments, and other negative credit information begin losing their negative effect after twelve months. Reviewing your credit report for accurate dates allows you to get rid of past negative events sooner.
- Check for indications you have been a victim of identity fraud. Search your report for names, social security numbers, and accounts that are not yours.

NOTE: some creditors "re-age" debt. This means a creditor may report negative information like bankruptcy, foreclosure, judgment, or collections as recently as today, as opposed to the true date. Re-aging is done for many reasons, from a simple reporting error to full manipulation by the creditor with the purpose of selling the "fresh debt" to debt collectors. Re-aging negative reports are something you need to be on the lookout for because it will significantly hurt your credit. If you find negative information has been re-aged, immediately work with that creditor and credit bureau to correct the error.

Credit Report Errors

The credit report is the key to building and improving your credit score. The quicker you build credit and show a strong twelve months of credit history, the quicker you can improve your credit score. However, excessive credit use, late or non-payments, and errors all hurt your credit score.

A credit report error can be as simple as having a repeated or duplicated collection account, wrong address, or wrong account name. Credit report errors can include reduced or missing credit limits, inflated credit balances, debts belonging to other people, multiple social security numbers, wrong addresses, and wrong or incorrect variations on your name.

Simply speaking, you can combine most credit errors into two groups: high priority and low priority credit errors. Since all credit scores are based solely on the credit report, removing high-priority errors will result in the quickest and most permanent improvements.

High-priority credit errors include inaccurate reporting of credit limits and balances owed. In order to build and strengthen your credit, it is important to show as high a credit limit as possible, with a balanced owed of no more than 30% of the credit limit. Other high-priority credit errors include an old bankruptcy being reported as filed within the last year.

Low priority credit errors include inaccurate reporting of irrelevant or helpful factors. Exaggerated credit limits will not hurt you. Repossession of an auto ten years ago, being reported as occurring eight years ago will not hurt your credit. Do not correct errors that are in your favor. Low-priority credit errors are not likely to hurt your credit score and can be ignored. Focus your time and resources on correcting high-priority negative errors.

High-Priority Credit Report Errors

- Collection notices are listed more than once (duplicates).
- Mistakes or errors in your payment history that occurred within the past two years.
- Missing or reduced account credit limits.
- Collection notices that are not yours.
- Incorrect information such as a current address, prior addresses, and current employer.
- Accounts that do not belong to you (this could indicate identity fraud or the beginning of your credit report is merged with another person's report).
- Someone else's social security number or a mistake in your social security number (this could indicate identity fraud or the beginning of your credit report is merged with another person's report).
- Someone else's name or a mistake in your name (this could indicate identity fraud or the beginning of your credit report being merged with another person's report).

Low-Priority Credit Report Errors

- Mistakes in your payment history that occurred more than two years ago.
- Delinquencies were older than seven years.
- Beneficial account inaccuracies (e.g., inflated credit limits).
- The wrong date of birth is a low priority error—unless you think you might be a victim of identity fraud.
- Typos in account numbers are a low priority—unless you believe you might be a victim of identity fraud.

Disputing Credit Report Errors

After reviewing each credit report, you find a high-priority credit error—what's next? You need to take action and get those errors deleted or corrected as quickly as possible. Begin by writing the offending credit bureau and the creditor directly. See the appendix called "credit dispute letter" for an example of a dispute letter, and the appendix called "how to get your free credit report" and "identity theft: how to report it" for credit bureau contact information. Be sure your letter specifies the error and be specific in how the error needs to be corrected, and request a letter confirming the action taken to be mailed to you.

Disputing an error with a credit bureau or creditor is free. Once you formally contact them, they will investigate the disputed claim and, if applicable, delete or correct the error. The following three steps are recommended when disputing an error with the credit bureaus:

Step One: Contact the Offending Credit Bureau

- It is possible that not all creditors report to all the credit bureaus. For this reason, only contact the credit bureau(s) that is reporting the erroneous negative credit information.
- Use the "credit report dispute letter—sample" found in the appendix.
- Explain in your letter what is inaccurate and give specific directions as to the corrective action you want to be taken.

- When possible, include proof in your letter to support the claim.
- Enclose a copy of the credit report, with the item(s) in question circled. (Make sure to send the credit report to the corresponding credit bureau.)
- The credit bureau is required to confirm with the creditor and investigate the disputed information within 30 days.
- The creditor is required by law to investigate the disputed data and report its findings.
- If the dispute results in a change to your credit report, the credit bureau will send you a written response and a free copy of your updated credit report.
- However, if the creditor disagrees with your claim, the credit bureau will mail you a written explanation stating the disputed item is accurate.

Step Two: Keep a Record

- Keep records of all phone and email communications.
- Keep copies of every letter sent and received.
- Keep proof supporting your claim—this can include anything from canceled payment checks to past billing statements.
- If you're missing key billing statements, the Fair Credit Billing Act requires each creditor to keep past statements on file which you can request for a fee.
- Call the billing or creditor registration department and ask what you need.

Step Three: Keep at It

Continue to check your credit reports once a year at the very least. Make sure no new derogatory or harmful errors or negative information has been added to your credit report, and the corrected errors have not been included in your credit record.

NOTE: you are not alone in this fight. As of 2012, you can now ask the federal government to help you fix credit report errors.

Chapter 7.   Credit Scoring and the Automobile Industry

Over the past few years, credit scoring has become a central part of the automotive industry. It was adopted as a standard way to determine if potential car buyers should be approved for loans or not. Currently, there is much contention and debate over this method.

Credit scoring is a system that assigns risk scores to individuals based on their past credit history. These scores are used to help banks or other lenders decide whether the individual should be approved for a loan, thus allowing them to charge higher interest rates when they need to. In order to understand how credit scoring works and what it has done for the automobile industry, one must first understand risk analysis.

Risk analysis is often used in business settings where there are many different variables that contribute towards an outcome like financial loss or success. For example, if a car were to be manufactured at a loss and sold, the manufacturer could lose a significant amount of money. If the manufacturer sells 100 cars for $5000 each but loses $500 on each car sold, they would incur a $50 000 loss for selling those 100 cars. However, if the cars were to be manufactured at a profit and sold for $10000 each, then the net profit would be around $50000.

Credit scoring is based on risk analysis in that it is used in order to determine how risky it would be to give someone credit. The more information a bank can gather about an individual, the more accurate their risk analysis can be. This is why credit scoring is useful because it can dramatically help inform lenders so they can make more informed loan decisions.

Credit scoring has become a method of measuring risk in almost every business sector as well as every industry (e.g., the automotive industry). While the majority of businesses will only utilize credit scoring systems in the financial sector, there are still many businesses that utilize credit scoring systems outside of their financial sector. For example, insurance agencies may use this system to decide whether or not individuals should be insured or how much an individual should pay depending on their insurance policy. Credit scoring affects the automobile industry in that if policyholders are considered at a high risk of defaulting on their payments, the interest rate will be increased. This is why credit scoring is so important to the auto industry.

How Credit Scoring Works

Credit score is made up of different numbers that are determined by using the information as well as factors of your personal life such as income, debt, housing status/amount you owe on your mortgage, length of time since you last paid on an outstanding balance, etc. It is all part of a complex process that lenders use to determine if they should approve or decline your request for a loan.

The Automobile Industry

In order to understand how credit scoring works and what it has done for the automobile industry, one must first understand risk analysis. In the past, car dealerships were just as susceptible to financial loss as a manufacturer losing money selling a car. However, with credit scoring now used by many car dealers in order to determine whether or not their customers will be able to make their payments in full and on time, more individuals can afford a car in these dealerships. This is good news for car dealers as they can now offer more cars at cheaper rates. As a result, there is a higher demand for the automobiles that are sold, causing the sector to expand.

Some of the ways credit scoring has helped to increase the automobile industry is by helping to attract new buyers to purchase more cars and trucks at dealerships. Today, many people are able to purchase their first car from a dealership since they do not need perfect credit scores to qualify for loans. Many of these buyers have not taken care of their payments on time in the past and are able to take advantage of dealerships offering them new cars at a lower, possibly even zero down payment, interest rate. As a result, the demand for new automobiles has increased. Though this is good news for buyers, it also has bad side effects as more people can purchase cars but there are also more cars on the road. Research shows that most people have a negative perception of driving in a large city vehicle and many choose to buy small, fewer models' vehicles rather than larger ones. But nowadays many individuals are able to purchase even smaller vehicles due to all the pickups they can afford from large companies like Ford and Toyota. This may seem like good news, except for when there are accidents involving these vehicles. Lower to reasonable models of vehicles will cause more accidents because these cars do not have the protective features that the larger cars do. This is why car dealerships should offer financing for customers with poor credit scores, but they should also be careful and make sure there is enough incentive offered by the automobile industry to prevent this from happening.

It is important today for car dealerships to offer customers with little to no credit history, but this presents a problem because what if they cannot pay their payments in full and on time? In order to combat this problem, many dealerships feel as though they must increase interest rates to avoid default rates. This is a negative side effect of communication and credit scoring because people who do not have good or perfect credit scores will not be able to get a car loan but will still find the price of a car to be very expensive. Due to these higher interest rates, the automobile industry is susceptible to financial loss and this can negatively affect workers in their sales offices because many customers hold onto their payments due to the higher interest rates.

Though it may appear that selling more automobiles to people with bad credit is a terrific way for automakers to generate more money, there are some negative implications that could affect society as a whole if everyone's rates are hiked. If more individuals are raising their rates due to credit scoring, then families who do not have good or perfect credit will be without a vehicle. Though this is a problem, it could also bring about an increase in the trucking industry so as to provide more people with trucks to travel in. As long as there are enough incentives offered for companies to build cars for everyone and continue to make cars at a cheap price, then the automobile industry will be fine and continue to grow. However, if more individuals purchase fewer cars and trucks, there is less fuel available on the market which could cause another effect on society as a whole: the price of oil would rise and then other fuels may require higher prices. This would make it more difficult for families to travel and find jobs in other states or cities due to the higher prices of fuel.

Although many people approve of the idea of credit scoring, some people do not because of the fact that it can "lead to discrimination in lending access" and "impose limits on consumers' credit access and the amount they can borrow and pay back" (Finnigan, et al). This is true because of the fact that people are given a rough estimation of their creditworthiness, and this can limit their access to mortgages, credit cards, and other kinds of loans. However, this is only if they do not receive help from one of the several agencies who can provide assistance for them to get through the process. This issue could be solved by offering affordable loans that will help individuals with bad credit histories earn money in order to afford living expenses and eventually start paying back their debts.

Another problem associated with the existence of credit scoring is that it "is considered a form of consumer profiling" (Finnigan, et al). Consumer profiling is an invasion of consumers' privacy and can lead to the "creation of discriminatory markets" (Finnigan, et al). For example, a credit score might only be available to people whose net worth is above a certain number.

This could lead to loan prejudice. However, this problem could also be solved by offering affordable loans that will help individuals with bad credit histories earn money in order to afford living expenses and eventually start paying back their debts. Many creditors are not willing to offer this and would rather simply discriminate.

Advantages of Credit Scoring vs Traditional Approval

Vehicle buyers who have a good credit score will most likely be approved for their loan. In comparison to those with poor credit, those with good credit are more likely to buy vehicles and also less likely to default on their payments as well as pay the lender back in time. With traditional approval, the lender typically checks the applicant's employment history, background (i.e., criminal record), and asset/liability ratios.

If the applicant is found to have a clean background and good employment history, the lender may approve the loan which can be very risky because if the borrower defaults on their payments, it is very difficult to collect on these payments. Employers usually do not keep a record of their employees' credit histories which makes it hard for lenders to know whether or not they can trust the applicant with a loan. A lender's job is to assess risk when approving loans, however, if there is no information readily available, then there will be no way for them to do so accurately (or at least as accurately as possible). Credit scoring has been suggested as a solution for this problem.

Credit Scoring and the Automobile Industry

"The rapid expansion in credit scoring as a problem-solving tool in the recent two decades has been impacted by changes in loan legislation, accounting standards, and technology," according to the Federal Reserve Bank of St. Louis. These forces have resulted primarily from an increased focus on the ability of borrowers to repay loans and reduce risks."

Automobile lenders are concerned with their ability to accurately assess risk. It is very risky for them to approve loans for those that do not have good credit because if the borrower defaults on payments or cannot afford their payments, it will be very difficult for them to collect on these payments. It is a lot easier for the lender to determine if you have good or bad credit depending on your score.

The Auto Finance Sector and Credit Scoring are meant to benefit the consumer. It allows them to assess risk in a more efficient way than before. However, some have argued that this method is not appropriate for assessing risk because it does not take other factors into account such as job stability and employment history which are still important in determining whether or not you can afford your loan payments and whether or not you will be able to pay back the amount that you owe.

Chapter 8. Properly Dispute Negative Account

Negative subtleties on your credit report are terrible glaring tokens of your past monetary slip-ups. Or on the other hand, at times, the misstep isn't yours; however, a business or credit agency is to be faulted for credit report mistakes. In any case, it's dependent upon you to work to have negative credit report sections expelled from your credit report.

Evacuating negative data will assist you with accomplishing a superior credit score. A superior credit report is likewise the way to getting endorsed for credit cards and advances and to getting great loan fees on the records that you're affirmed for. To help with your approach to all the more likely credit, here are a few procedures to get negative credit report data expelled from your credit report.

Present a Dispute to the Credit Bureau

Credit report debates are most effortless when made on the web or through the mail. To make a debate on the web, you should have, as of late, arranged a duplicate of your credit report. You can present a question to the credit department who gave the credit report.

To debate by means of mail, compose a letter portraying the credit report and submit duplicates of any confirmation you have. The credit department examines your contest with the business that gave the data and expels the passage if they find that is, in reality, a blunder.

Contest with the Business That Reported to the Credit Bureau

Presently, you can totally sidestep the credit department and debate straightforwardly with the business that revealed the mistake to the credit authority, e.g., the credit card guarantor, bank, or obligation gatherer. You can make the contest recorded as a hard copy, and the business is required to do an examination simply like the credit bureau.

When the business establishes that there's to be sure a blunder on your credit report, they should notify all the credit departments of that mistake so your credit reports can be adjusted.

Send a Pay for Delete Offer to Your Creditor

You need to move toward precisely detailed negative data differently. Credit agencies won't expel exact, verifiable data regardless of whether you question it (because the examination will verify the exactness of this data), so you may need to haggle to have a few things expelled from your credit report.

Pay-for-erase offer is a method you can use with the reprobate or past due accounts. In a pay-for-erase arrangement, you offer to cover the record in return for having the negative subtleties expelled from your credit report. A few creditors will take you up on the offer.

Make a Goodwill Request for Deletion

With pay-for-erase, you can utilize cash as the negotiating concession for getting negative data expelled from your credit report. If you've just paid the record, be that as it may, you don't have much arranging power. Now, you can request kindness by mentioning a generosity deletion.

In a letter to the creditor, you may depict why you were late, state how you've since been a decent paying client, and ask that the records be accounted for much better. Once more, creditors don't need to consent and some won't. Then again, a few creditors will make these erasures if you converse with the correct individual.

Hold up Out the Credit Reporting Time Limit

If all else fizzles, your lone decision is to trust that those negative things will tumble off your credit report. Luckily, the law just permits the most negative data to be accounted for seven years. The special case is liquidation, which can be accounted for up to 10 years. The other uplifting news is that negative data influences your credit scoreless as it gets more established and as you supplant it with positive data. The holdup may not be as difficult as you might suspect. Buyers can demand their own credit report for nothing like clockwork from the three significant revealing organizations. In this way, no doubt, you should demand a report after the maturing time frame to affirm.

It is essential to note, in any case, that while the credit detailing organization will commonly erase the negative data from the report after the seven-year maturing period, data may, in any case, be kept on a document and can be discharged in specific situations. Those conditions incorporate when going after a position that pays over a specific sum, or applying for a credit line or a life protection strategy worth over a specific sum. Contingent upon where you live there might be progressively positive guidelines under state law, for example, a shorter legal time limit. You should contact your state's Attorney General's office for more data.

Meanwhile, you can improve your credit by making convenient installments on accounts you despite everything have open and dynamic.

What Doesn't Work

Petitioning for financial protection doesn't expel negative data from your credit report. If and when your obligations are released, the parities will be accounted as $0, however, the records will stay on your credit report. Also, accounts that were remembered for your insolvency will be noted all things considered.

Shutting a record won't kill the wrongdoing announcing. If you close a record with a past due to equalization, your installment will even now be accounted as reprobate until you get up to speed with the payment. The main thing shutting a record does is shield you from utilizing it.

Paying a reprobate parity doesn't delete the negative section on your credit report. When you pay the equalization, the record status will change to "current" or "all right" as long as the record isn't charged-off or in assortments. Charge-offs and assortment records will keep on being accounted for that path considerably after you pay the parity.

How to get rid of blunders on your report

Blunders on purchaser credit reports can be a typical event. That commits realizing how to debate an error on your credit report significant. If you discover something in your credit report that doesn't have a place there, this is what to do.

Stage 1 – Identify any credit report blunders

Audit your credit reports occasionally for wrong or deficient data. At annualcreditreport.com, you may acquire one free credit report from each of the three major credit bureaus—Equifax, Experian, and TransUnion—once a year. You can also purchase, usually at a cost, a credit checking service and analyze your report on a monthly basis.

Some basic credit report blunders you may spot include:

- Character errors, for example, an off-base name, telephone number, or address.
- A purported blended document that contains account data having a place with another customer. This may happen when you and another shopper have the equivalent or comparative names.
- A record erroneously credited to you because of data fraud.
- A shut record that is as yet being accounted for as open.
- An inaccurate detailing of you as a record proprietor, when you are only an approved client on a record.
- A record that is erroneously marked as late or reprobate, which could incorporate obsolete data, for example, a late installment that is more than 7 years of age or a mistaken date with respect to your last installment.
- A similar obligation was recorded more than once.
- A record registered more than once with different creditors.
- Wrong record adjusts.
- Mistaken credit limits.

How a Blunder on Your Credit Report Can Influence You

Is it extremely important to keep close tabs on your credit report? Can one mistake truly affect you? Indeed. Your credit report provides a wealth of information about you, such as how you manage your debts and if you've ever applied for financial assistance. You could be affected adversely by a mistake on your credit report from numerous points of view.

To begin, comprehend that credit revealing organizations sell the data in your credit reports to bunches that incorporate bosses, back up plans, service organizations, and numerous different gatherings that need to utilize that data to verify your character and assess your creditworthiness.

For example, if a service organization surveys your credit history and finds a not exactly ideal credit report, they may offer fewer good terms to you as a client. While this is called hazard-based evaluating and organizations must notify you if they're doing this, it can, in any case, affect you. Your credit report additionally may influence whether you can get an advance and the provisions of that advance, including your financing cost.

Stage 2 — Contact the furnisher
Your subsequent stage is to contact the furnisher or the organization that gave the wrong data, which could be an element like your bank or a service organization. Verify their records and affirm the mistake. You might have the option to determine the issue now. If the issue can't be settled, contact the credit detailing department straightforwardly.

Stage 3 – Credit Report's Errors
Under the Fair Credit Reporting Act, both the credit announcing agency and the organization that reports the data about you to the credit department are required to acknowledge questions from buyers—and right any wrong or inadequate data about you in that report.

The U.S. Government Trade Commission (FTC) suggests taking these activities:

- Tell the credit authority, recorded as a hard copy, what data you believe is mistaken. The Federal Trade Commission gives an example contest letter that makes this progression simpler. The letter traces what data to incorporate, from introducing the realities to mentioning that the blunder be expelled or remedied.

- Incorporate duplicates, not firsts, of materials that help your position.
- Consider encasing a duplicate of your credit report with the mistakes circumnavigated or featured.
- Send your letter by certified mail with "return receipt mentioned"—to guarantee the letter is conveyed. Keep your mail station receipt.
- Keep duplicates of all that you send.

Where to Send Your Contest Letter

Send your credit report contest letter to the credit announcing authority, just as to the organization that revealed the wrong data about you.

Stage 4 – Allow time for the examination

Credit revealing agencies must examine the contested things. The procedure, as a rule, takes less than 30 days. They're required to send important data to the data supplier—which means, whoever detailed the contested thing. The supplier must research the debate and report back to the credit announcing department.

If you're correct—and it is a blunder—the data supplier needs to notify the three significant credit authorities so they can address the data in your credit reports.

A Pointless Credit Report Contest

The credit agency or the organization that gave the data (the furnisher) likewise can verify that your case is negligible, in which matter they can choose not to research your case. In any case, they hould tell you they've declined to examine your question by composing a notification within five days.

Chapter 9.   The Truth About Credit Bureaus

Credit Bureaus are among the few organizations that can help you shape what happens in your financial world. Their presence, accuracy, errors, and general policies can affect your chances of getting financial support affect any person or firm in the world today. Without mincing words, it is okay not to understand religious organizations, social organizations, or certain niches in the business world. But Credit bureaus? Nobody gets far in the business world without them. It is even wrong to start taking up loans and credits without having vital information on companies like these, and that's why I will tell you about them now. You will learn how vital they are to your credit too.

For a start, what exactly is a credit bureau? A credit bureau is a well-established organization that is saddled with the job of keeping and supplying related information on your credit every time you need it. They are usually called Credit Reporting Agencies because that's the top of what they do; report your credit. Credit bureaus or credit reporting agencies are usually specialized companies or organizations that take up the job of collecting, compiling, and providing every necessary information on your credit when you need it. This is usually packed up and reported in the document formally known as 'credit report'.

Now, what is a credit report? It's a well-researched compilation of facts about your credit. The research is all done by your credit bureau; they only provide the details when you need them. They provide all related information that may help you decide how well you have handled your credit information. That would include some statistics such as your personal information, your credit information (the firms you have drawn credits with and what types of credit you have drawn), the previous judgments you have had based on finance, and your current credit score. You already have a good idea of what comprises your credit score.

Your credit reporting agencies are expected to provide you a free credit report once a year, and they may produce more than one on a charged basis. You may write to them to provide your credit information to certain companies. Usually, credit companies with which you are in a transaction already or from which you are about obtaining some credit. Credit Bureaus may provide your credit information when ordered by a court or the government, and definitely, your insurance company naturally gets a copy apart from cases where overviews of credit information are used in researches.

Your Credit Bureau would usually begin operation the instant you create a profile with them, and you instruct your credit companies to forward details of your credit transactions to them. For instance, you create a credit profile with TransUnion, a notable credit reporting agency in the United States. Then, you instruct your credit card companies to forward reports of your transaction with them to TransUnion, your credit Bureau. This means you expect your credit card company to supply reports on the type of loan you have drawn with them, how well you can pay up, and their overall impression of your payment style. Such information would be supplied with your full name, the time you drew the loans, the time you are expected to pay it all, and clauses you have added during the deal. They are not expected to speak in your favor or against you, but only supply the information they gather about your interaction to the credit bureau.

It is the same thing when you take secured loans, you surely remember credit cards offer unsecured loans. If you draw up a student loan, mortgage, or any other type of debt you may refer to as good or bad debt, you are drawing a secured loan. You may instruct your lenders to forward details of your transaction with them too. It is not necessary, but it is always advised since the next lender will likely lend you based on how impressed they are when they read and verify your previous debts, particularly how well you handled your last debt. The whole idea of credit scores and credit reporting centers on that.

Credit Bureaus do not collect all of your information, but are particular about only the pieces that relate to your credit, which will include statistics like "from whom did you draw credits, what were the policies agreed upon, what were the terms and how did you stick by them?" Your credit Bureaus then compile all of these bits and grade you on your performance in each and all of them. Some formats are followed when grading a credit report, and we will talk about every one of them in due time.

But we might begin by revealing more about the credit bureaus themselves. According to National Finance, there are three major credit reporting agencies in the US, they are TransUnion, Experian, and Equifax. American Bankers also report that these three are backed by different credit Acts in the US and they may request your credit records, your financial history, and certain personal information that may help them trace and compact your performance in credit dealings, even without informing you. Let's read up a bit on them:

1. TransUnion: If you'd like to judge them by the number of people they cover, TransUnion is the smallest of the three credit bureaus that are recognized in the United States, but it holds the widest range. It covers no less than 30 different countries in the world, including the United Kingdom. It provides demographic data and analytics alongside credit reports, and it is considered among the most reliable of the credit bureaus in the world. By 2020, TransUnion would be 52 years since establishment.
2. Experian: Experian was established only 23 years ago (as of 2019), so it is usually considered the youngest of the three by age. But nonetheless, Experian stands among the most reliable credit reporting agencies in the country. It is most popular in countries across Europe and of course the United States, and it has headquarters in world countries. It renders the same services as TransUnion, and it records information on more than 200 million citizens in the US alone.
3. Equifax: The oldest largest and most popular in the United States, Equifax is the third of the main credit companies recognized in the US. It keeps the record of well over 800 million people, besides millions of business profiles. Equifax holds an impressive record of credit keeping across all states in the US, and as such, it is often recognized as others.

According to American Bankers, the three organizations are charged with three major assignments — collecting your information, making an analysis of what they got, and making that available to due companies, and certainly, yourself. Every other credit bureau is charged with the same assignment, but it is worthy of note that about 100 other credit bureaus exist, only that they are rarely accessible to all citizens.

Each of these credit bureaus is expected to provide a free credit report to each individual on request. They must also present an avenue through which citizens may refute and challenge the statistics in their credit report. This means that if you receive your credit report and you observe some statistics that have doubts about, you may reach your credit bureau and have the error corrected.

How does your credit reporting agency get reports on your credit?

Credit bureaus require information, and they need to find it in some way. It is the only way they can have enough records to provide when you request your credit information, and they are protected by the Fair Credit Reporting Act in the US. This Act grants them the license to collect information on everyone they can and compile this information with the SS Number of each person. It is interesting to note that each agency has its method of getting information. This is why certain information may reflect in the report of a company and may be missing in the report of others.

Generally, what exactly do they need about you and how should they get your information?

The information credit bureaus usually require include:

1. Your data: The immediate data with which you want to be recognized is important. Your full name, your financial history, your social security number, and so forth. It has to match with what you have got on other papers. Credit bureaus try to see to it that your information is genuinely yours, and information belonging to someone with a similar name is not mixed up. It is worthy of note that credit companies or credit

bureaus do not require your bank account details, your income scale, or such statistics. They are only interested in what directly accounts for your credit.

2. Your credit information: This is other important information the credit bureau set out to collect. Your credit bureau gathers your credit history, your past and present credit deals, and your commitment to each of them, as well as the rate at which your credit information can influence your credit score. It actually determines how high or low your credit score is, alongside a few other features.

3. Public Judgment: Public judgment can be an eye-opener for lending companies. If you have been vindicated in many court cases, it may prove to lenders that you are a brilliant debtor who must be venerated. It may also be the reason your lenders are skeptical if they realize you have poor public judgments, you have defaulted on many loans and you had to result to a range of alternatives before them.

4. Recent Inquiries: Lastly, the total number of firms that have recently inquired about your credit report is included in the credit report. The names and profiles of the firms, the form of deal you propose to them, and so on are bits of information that your credit reporting agency may also set out to find.

So, how do they find all this data?

1. From your creditors: The most certain source of information is your creditors. They have records of how you performed in your debts. They usually submit a regular update on all of their clients to the credit bureaus, except in cases when the debtor requests that their credit information should not be sent to a credit bureau. In other cases, you may have to notify your credit company to supply your credit bureau with your credit information. Besides, public judgments and your recent inquiries, your credit companies usually supply the main information your firm is simple. Usually, your creditors are Credit Unions or banks.

2. The court: The court is another reliable source of information. The court provides a variety of information, ranging from public judgments to records of foreclosure,

bankruptcy, and similar situations. The court naturally provides this information to the public record, and also sends them to credit bureaus the instant they are updated.

Chapter 10. How Your Credit Repair Score Is Calculated

The credit score is calculated using several pieces of your credit report. If you want to have a high credit score or have good credit, you must know how it is calculated and what factors (banks and credit agencies) must approve or deny a loan or credit card.

Your credit score is calculated based on these categories, namely:

- The amounts that you owe
- The history of Payment
- What types of open accounts you have
- The age of the accounts
- The number of credit applications

Let's examine these factors and see how we can raise your credit score one by one.

The Amounts That You Owe

It is no coincidence that the amounts you owe are the next thing to discuss. This is because, after the history of payment, it is known to be the next most influencing factor of your credit score.

It is already a general rule that you are required to use only 30% of the credit the bank approves and nothing more than that. It will be highly unwise if you use all the credit that the bank approves, say $300 on a $1000 credit card. That means you should never make use of the maximum account allowed on your card.

Credit bureaus perceive this as an omen when you start to depend on the money, and they tend to withdraw as it signifies a negative mark for your credit report and your credit score.

I would advise you to use below 30% of your credit, or what's best is you could go ahead to use only 10% of your credit line and nothing more than that. By doing this, you will have better credit scores, and your chances of increasing and even sustaining a good credit score will be limitless.

The amount of money you owe is also a key factor to consider when calculating your score.

The History of Payment

Consider making payments on or even earlier than the agreed time, as it is absolutely important and has a major impact on your score. If you make late payments, then your credit score will dramatically reduce.

The fundamental thing a lender would want to find out is whether or not you paid your bills or even your credit loans in good time. This category, out of the others, majorly influences your credit score and makes up to 35% of your score, which is why it is very important to take note of it.

Now that you know that delayed payments can affect your credit score and hinder you from building a good credit history, you must ensure you pay all debts on time without any qualms.

The types of accounts normally considered for payment history are namely:

- Installment Loans
- Credit Cards (such as Visa, Master Card, and so on)
- Loans to the consumer
- Retail accounts and;
- Mortgage Loans

Remember, making and building a good credit score is a path that will require you to make payments on time.

What Types of Open Accounts You Have?

Another factor that can favor your credit score is having various types of loans (mortgages, cars, and student loans) and credit cards.

Your credit score is majorly concerned with the different types of credit you use, some of which exist are credit cards, mortgage loans, installment loans, and accounts with finance companies.

Note that it is not so important that you use each one of them, and I'll advise that you only open accounts that you are going to use.

The credit mix has no major effect on your credit score, but it is of great importance that your credit report does not contain excess information on which your score is based.

There is no perfect version of a credit mix as it varies with time from individual to individual. Opening car loans, student loans, and credit cards you won't be needing won't be advisable for you.

It would be an added advantage to have this factor that shows that you know how to handle your credit responsibly.

The Age of the Accounts

Consistency is key in the credit score world. As long as you keep maintaining a good credit score history, your credit score will always remain high. The general rule of thumb explains this because the longer you have credit cards, the more your credit score will increase. That's why I'll advise you to start your credit as soon as you can. This is a factor that constitutes about 15% of your credit score, measuring the length at which you have your credit accounts and how well you have managed them within that period.

Here is what your FICO credit score records:

- It considers the age of both the new and old accounts and even the average age of all of your accounts.
- It also considers your credit lines (if you have), how long you have been with them and how your payment history has been.

- Finally, it measures your loans/credit cards' exact age. Because of this, many professionals advise that older accounts should neither be closed nor canceled, as it is likely to affect your credit score.

There's a high possibility of you having a high credit score by having a long time with your credit.

The Number of Credit Applications

Lastly, the number of applications to your credit slightly affects your credit score. Every time you apply for a loan or possibly a credit card (even if not yet approved), your credit score slightly decreases.

Opening various credit accounts within a very short time can be very risky for financial institutions, especially when it's a case of one who does not have a lengthy credit history. This explains why many people see that their credit score has decreased either when they open a credit card or when they are approved for a particular loan. However, the decline is temporary.

Also, bear in mind that credit checks vary. Interestingly, checking your credit will have your credit score reduced if and only if it is a hard inquiry. There are hard inquiries and soft inquiries, which I will explain below.

A hard inquiry is made when a loan is applied to a lender. That may include a student loan, car, mortgage loan. These inquiries affect your credit score.

While the soft inquiry is made when you request a copy of your credit report, apply for a job, or use it for a credit monitoring service. These types of inquiries in no way affect your credit score.

How Exactly Is It Calculated?

As important as it is to calculate your credit score, it is also very important to know that these factors have no fixed percentage. They may vary due to the financial information obtained from your credit report.

This goes to say that without adequate knowledge of the basic factors above, there is a tendency for an individual to be careless in the decisions he makes at obtaining a high credit score. It is hence very important that these factors are known.

Though these factors are applied when calculating a credit report, the level of importance varies from person to person.

It is not possible to record the impact of each factor on the credit score without acknowledging the report as a whole.

How to Check Your Credit Score

Some services enable you to check your credit score at very little or no cost. However, you must take caution and use services that you know are reliable so that you don't fall into the hands of scammers on the Internet. Some of these reliable services, especially those listed below, have no cost.

Chapter 11.   The Fico Credit Scores

Fair Isaac Corporation—the business that produces "FICO" ratings—is the oldest and most omnipresent credit scoring agency. Fair Isaac claims over 80% of investors use their ratings. Factors considered by Fair Isaac as credit scores come up include:

- Payment history (about 35% of the score): the company is looking at things like whether you have paid on time, have any overdue payments, declared bankruptcy, how current past due accounts are, or if you have rulings against you. This is the bulk of your score, so it's the most important. Late payments, settlement claims, settled accounts, repossessions, foreclosures, and public record issues such as tax liens, convictions, or bankruptcies can have a significant negative impact on your FICO score, according to Fair Isaac. Even getting a payment just one month late can have a negative impact on your ranking.
- Amounts owed on credit accounts (about 30% of the score): FICO looks at things like the amounts that you be obliged, and how many of your accounts hold a balance. The principal way to improve this part of your score is to pay down your outstanding debt. Your credit history has a period of around 15% of the score. Longer credit history usually yields a higher ranking.
- New credit (about 10% of the score): Fair Isaac wants to see a credit history built rather than a lot of new accounts. Opening up multiple accounts in a short time may mean a higher risk. Depending on the reason, hard inquiries about your account may also lower your score. For example, if your credit report is reviewed by a variety of borrowers, it might seem like you are actively applying for new credit. That is why, when shopping for new credit, it is important to be careful. Above all, used car dealers always want to get you to sign a form that requires them to peek at your credit report, even if you're just shopping in the store. Don't consider that until you are adamant about entering into an agreement. But as long as you're doing all of your car or home mortgage comparison shopping within about 30 days or so, it shouldn't have a lot of

effect on your ranking. Don't think about inquiries too much, they make up just a small fraction of your FICO score. According to FICO, the number of requests is typically not a major factor in your credit score— an investigation will probably lower your score by less than 5 points, even if outside a small shopping window for reference. So, FICO states that once the investigation is longer than 12 months it does not include inquiries in its ratings.

- Types of credit (about 10% of the score): Fair Isaac is offering a "healthy mix" of different credit forms, including revolving loans (such as credit cards) and maintenance plans (such as a mortgage or car loan). You can see that about 65% of your FICO score depends on whether you pay your bills on time (35%) and whether the balance you owe is too high for your credit limits (30%). You may have more than one FICO score as Fair Isaac now provides a number of FICO rating models that highlight different aspects of your performance, and because a FICO score is dependent on your credit report, and each of the three national credit reporting agencies may have very different information on you, the ratings may vary from each of the three organizations.

What Is a Good FICO Score?

FICO scores range between 300 and 850. Fair Isaac reports that just fewer than 40% of Americans have more than 750 FICO ratings, which most borrowers would find very strong. Equifax claims most FICO scores usually fall between the 600s and 700s and offers these estimates:

- 20% are above 780.
- 20% are in the range of 745–780.
- 20% are in the range of 690–745.
- 20% are in the range of 620–690.
- 20% are below 619.

Fair Isaac offers a free calculator that you can use to see how different credit ratings can influence how much you're getting credit for. Go to www.myfico.com and click "Education," then "Credit basics," then scroll down on the left and click "Improve your score," then click on "See how much money you can save" in the article.

Most Common Reasons for Negative Credit Decisions

Underneath are the most common reasons for negative credit decisions, according to Equifax. You can see how these fit in with the way you score credit files.

- Serious offense.
- Extreme delinquency and a filed or triggered public record.
- It is too new or uncertain since the offense.
- The level of account criminality is too high.
- The percentage of delinquency accounts is too high.
- Money owed too high on deposits.
- The percentage of credit-limit balances to revolving accounts is too high.
- The length of time the account is set is too short.
- Too many balance accounts.

The FICO Scoring Model

FICO has the reputation of being the most trustworthy scoring model, given its extensive track record. The Fair Isaac Company started calculating these values in 1989. They've updated the algorithms several times over the last three decades to account for changing factors and ensure that they continue to yield consistent credit ratings.

The standard FICO score approach will give you a score between 300 and 850. A score of less than 600 is considered low. It is considered exceptional if your score is greater than 740. Between 600 to 740, creditworthiness varies from medium to above-average.

FICO debuted its FICO 9 scoring model in 2014. The main change in this model was to downplay the significance of unpaid medical expenses. The explanation for this is that unpaid medical debts are not true financial health indicators. You could be waiting for insurance to pay a medical payment, or you could be completely uninformed that medical debt has been sent to a collection agency. For some people, this important change allowed their credit score to increase by up to 25 points.

Other amendments made in 2017 made it illegal for collectors to report late medical bills that were not yet 180 days past due. The three credit reporting bureaus also removed all data on civil judgments and tax lien records from their systems in 2017. According to FICO, this improved the scores of about 6% of individuals.

FICO 8 (which the company developed in 2009) was the standard credit-score version before FICO 9. The FICO 8 score is still the most widely used in the lending business. The differentiating elements of FICO 8 were that it penalized you for charging near your total credit limit each month and granted you forgiveness if you had only one 30-day late payment.

It's worth mentioning that when FICO updates its scoring algorithms, lenders have the option of keeping their current version or upgrading. Because upgrading to the new model is so expensive, FICO 8 has remained the clear preference. Even FICO 5 models are still used by some lenders. During the application process, you can inquire about the model your lender is employing.

In most cases, FICO ratings do not alter significantly in the short term. If you start missing payments or showing charge-offs and defaults, this is an exception. FICO scores aren't available to everyone. If you don't have credit, you'll be classified as "credit invisible," according to experts.

To get a FICO score, you must have six months of payments recorded to the credit bureaus.

What Is a FICO Score?

The credit score structure was formulated by the Fair Isaac Corporation also referred to as FICO. This credit score is utilized by financial institutions. There are other credit score models; however, the FICO score is the one that is most commonly used. Consumers can get and keep high credit scores by simply making sure their debt level remains low, and they maintain an extended history of paying their bills as and when they are due.

In the FICO scoring formula, not all credit reports are scored equally. Credit scores are weighted based on the particular "scorecard" that a person falls under. For example, if the person has filed for bankruptcy, they may be scored using a special "bankruptcy" scorecard. The credit score for a person under one scorecard may be affected differently by a negative event, like a late payment, than of someone with the same event on a different scorecard.

The scorecard you're on is determined by the most recent significant event in your credit history. The first 10 scorecards go something like this:

Scorecards 1–5:

1. Those with public records, including judgments and bankruptcy, on their credit report.
2. For those with serious delinquencies other than bankruptcies (60, 90, 120 latest, collections, judgments, charge-offs repossessions, etc.).
3. Those with only 1 credit account (very thin files).
4. Those with only 2 credit accounts (thin files).
5. Those with 3 credit accounts only.

Scorecards 6–10 should not have any grave felonies (the definition of "serious" is unknown).

6. 0–2 year's oldest account.
7. 2–5 year's oldest account.
8. 5–12 year's oldest account.
9. 12–19 year's oldest account.
10. 19+ years oldest account.

There is a total of 12 scorecards, and they are subject to change as FICO (formerly Fair Isaac Corp) updates its scoring formula.

Chapter 12.   Simple Steps to Fix Your Credit Scores

Improving your credit score can mean qualifying for lower financing costs and better terms. That is genuine whether you need a decent credit score to acquire cash for individual reasons (a home advance, a vehicle advance, to get a credit card, and so forth) or so you can buy stock, rent an office, and so on, to begin or develop your business.

The issue is, credit fix is similar to improving your expert system: You possibly consider it when it is important. However, if you don't have great credit, it's almost difficult to address that circumstance short-term.

That is the reason an opportunity to begin fixing your credit is currently - before you truly need it.

Luckily, it's not too difficult to improve your credit score.

Here's a basic procedure you can follow:

1. Audit your credit reports.

The credit authorities - TransUnion, Equifax, and Experian - are required to give you a free duplicate of your report once every year. You should simply inquire. (Snap the connections to demand a duplicate.)

Another approach to see your credit reports is to utilize free assistance like Credit Karma. (I'm not supporting Credit Karma. I like it and believe it's convenient. However, I'm certain other free administrations are similarly as valuable.)

When you've joined, you can see your credit scores and view the data contained on the reports. As a rule, the passages on the different reports will be the equivalent, however not generally. For an assortment of reasons, credit reports are infrequently indistinguishable.

2. Debate negative imprints.

In the past times, you needed to compose letters to the credit departments if you needed to question blunders. Presently benefits like Credit Karma (once more, I'm not supporting CK and just reference it because I've utilized it) let you contest blunders on the web.

Simply ensure you get the most blast for your debate endeavors. Certain variables gauge more vigorously on your credit score than others, so focus on those things first.

Start with critical imprints like assortment records and decisions. It's normal to have at any rate one assortment account show up on your report. I had two from medicinal services suppliers I utilized subsequent to having a cardiovascular failure; my insurance agency continued asserting it had paid while the suppliers said it had not, and in the long run the records wound up with an assortment organization. In the long run, I chose to pay the suppliers and contend with the insurance agency later. However, the two assortments ended up on my credit report.

Fixing those issues was simple. I tapped the "Contest" button, chose "The creditor consented to evacuate my obligation on this record," and inside seven days the debate was settled and the passage was expelled from my credit report.

You can likewise contest mistakes through each credit department. If that is your inclination, go here for TransUnion, here for Equifax, and here for Experian.

Remember a few questions will take longer than others. In any case, that is OK. When you start a contest, you're done: The credit departments are required to research it and report the goals.

Invest as much energy as it takes attempting to have deprecatory imprints expelled because they additionally weigh intensely on your general score.

3. Contest inaccurate late-installment sections.

Errors occur. Your home loan bank may report an installment was late that was in actuality paid on schedule. A credit card supplier may neglect to enter an installment accurately.

You can contest late installments - regardless of whether in accounts that are present or records that have been shut - a similar way you debate deprecatory imprints.

Your installment history is another factor that weighs vigorously on your credit score, so make a solid effort to tidy up those mistakes.

4. Choose if you need to play the game some credit fix organizations play.

So far, we've talked about attempting to expel off base data as it were. You can, if you pick, likewise debate exact data.

For instance, say a record went to assortment, you never paid it, and the assortment organization surrendered. All that remaining parts are the passage on your credit report. You can even now decide to debate the section. Numerous individuals do. What's more, in some cases those sections will get evacuated.

Why? When you enter a question the credit authority requests that the creditor verify the data. Some will. Many, similar to assortment offices, won't. They'll basically overlook the solicitation - and if they do disregard the solicitation, the office is required to expel the passage from your credit report.

This means littler firms, similar to assortment organizations or nearby loan specialists or little to average size specialist organizations, are less inclined to react to the credit departments. It's an issue they needn't bother with. Banks, credit card organizations, automobile fund organizations, and home loan moneylenders are much bound to react.

So, if you need - and I'm not suggesting this, I'm trying to say it's a system a few people choose to utilize - you can contest data in the expectation the creditor won't react. (This is the methodology many credit fix firms use to attempt to improve their customers' scores.) If the creditor doesn't react, the passage gets expelled.

5. Ask pleasantly.

Possibly you attempted and neglected to evacuate a negative remark, a late installment, or a record that was checked "Paid as concurred" (which may mean the creditor consented to let you pay short of what you owed). Would it be advisable for you to surrender? Not a chance. Take a stab at asking pleasantly.

Creditors can educate credit agencies to expel sections from your credit report whenever. For instance, I hadn't charged anything on a specific credit card for quite a long time and didn't see that I had been charged my yearly expense until the installment was late. (Like a good for nothing, I was simply hurling the announcements without opening them because I "knew" there were no charges.)

The late installment appeared on my credit report, so I called the credit card organization, clarified what had occurred, that I had been a client for quite a long time, and inquired as to whether they would expel the section. They said sure. Furthermore, they additionally consented to forgo every single yearly charge later on. (Demonstrating once more that if you don't ask, you don't get.)

When all else comes up short, call and ask pleasantly. You'll be amazed by how often a courteous solicitation for help pays off.

6. Increment credit limits.

Another factor that weighs intensely on your credit score is your credit card usage: The proportion of accessible credit to credit utilized has a major effect. As a rule, conveying a parity of in excess of 50 percent of your accessible credit will contrarily affect your score. Maximizing your cards will hurt your score.

One approach to improve your proportion is to square away your equalizations. However, another route is to expand your credit limit. If you owe $2,500 on a card with a $5,000 cutoff and you get the limit expanded to $7,500, your proportion immediately improves.

To get credit limits expanded, call and ask pleasantly. If you have a nice installment history, most credit card organizations will gladly build your breaking point - all things considered, they need you to convey a high parity. That is the manner by which they bring in cash.

Simply ensure you don't really utilize the extra accessible credit, because then you'll be back in the equivalent accessible credit proportion pontoon... also, you'll be more profound paying off debtors.

7. Open another credit card account.

Another approach to expand your credit card usage proportion is to open another record. For whatever length of time that you don't convey an equalization on that card, your accessible credit quickly increments by that card's breaking point.

Attempt to get a card that doesn't charge a yearly expense, however. Your most solid option is through a bank where you as of now have a record. Without a doubt, cards with no yearly expense will in general charge higher loan fees. However, if you never convey an equalization, the financing cost is unessential.

Be that as it may, once more, be keen: The objective isn't to gain admittance to more money, the objective is to improve your credit score. If you think you'll be enticed to run up an equalization on another record, don't open one.

8. Pay down extraordinary adjusts.

I know. You need a higher credit score because you need to acquire cash; if you had the cash to square away your parities, then you won't have to obtain it.

As yet: diminishing your level of accessible credit utilized can make a brisk and significant effect on your credit score. So go on a no-frills financial plan to let loose money to settle your equalization. Or on the other hand, sell something.

Squaring away adjusts might be hard to pull off as a transient move to expand your credit score, yet it ought to be a piece of your drawn-out monetary arrangement. Not exclusively will your credit score increment after some time, you won't pay as much premium - which, if you consider it, is simply giving moneylenders cash you would prefer remained in your pocket.

9. Pay off high-intrigue, "new" credit accounts first.

Time of credit matters to your credit report. Financing costs matter to your ledger. If you have $100 every month to put toward squaring away adjusts (far beyond the necessary regularly scheduled installments, obviously), center around taking care of high intrigue accounts. Then organize those by the age of the record. Pay off the most up-to-date ones first; that way you'll build the normal length of credit, which should support your score, yet you'll additionally have the option to all the more rapidly abstain from paying moderately high intrigue.

Then put the cash not spent on that installment into the following record on your rundown. The "obligation snowball" framework truly accomplishes work.

10. Ride some extraordinary credit coattails (of an individual you trust.)

State your life partner has a credit card with practically zero parity and an incredible installment history; if the individual in question consents to include you as an approved client, from a credit score perspective you consequently advantage from her card's accessible credit just as her installment history.

Remember if the individual in question makes a late installment, that passage will show up as negative on your credit report as well.

So, pick your credit card companions carefully.

11. Keep your "old" credit cards.

Your period of credit history has a moderate yet at the same time important effect on your credit score. Let's assume you've had a specific credit card for a long time; shutting that record may diminish your general normal credit history and adversely sway your score, particularly over the present moment.

If you're planning to expand your credit score however you additionally need to dispose of a credit card account, dispose of your "most up to date" card.

12. Cover each tab on schedule.

Indeed, even one late installment can hurt your score. Do all that you can, from this day on, to consistently cover your tabs on schedule.

What's more, if one month you can't pay everything on schedule, be keen about which charges you pay late. Your home loan moneylender or credit card supplier will report a late installment to the credit departments, yet utilities and cell suppliers likely won't.

Check the "Records" segment on your credit reports to see which records are recorded and if you need to pay late, pick a record that doesn't show up on your report.

Then make a solid effort to ensure you can generally pay everything on time later on. Your credit score will thank you, thus will your feelings of anxiety.

What's more, after some time, so will your financial balance.

Chapter 13.   Is Credit Repair Ethical?

Many people struggle to pay their debts and have insufficient or poor credit scores. Credit repair would be an option for them if they knew how it worked or what the risks are. There are plenty of people who claim credit repair is unethical, but no studies have been made on whether or not this type of process is actually against the law."

Is Credit Repair Ethical?

The topic of "credit repair" has become more prevalent in society over recent years, as a lot more people struggle with debt and lack of credit. Dave Askin claims that credit repair is unethical, and books such as The Credit Repair Manual claim that it is against the law too.

Is credit Repair Legal?

The problem with credit repair is that many people don't trust parts of it as they believe they are using parts of credit repair services for illegal purposes. It's important to understand what is legal and what isn't, in order to be able to make informed decisions about your personal finances. Whether or not a particular company claims to offer an "ethical" process (whatever that means) or not really doesn't matter. You must be aware of the fact that nothing can absolutely be 100% ethical or legal in this world.

Credit Repair vs. Credit Rating

There are two different things that you need to understand /undefined [before] you can make a decision about how much credit repair is ethical for you. The first one is a credit rating. A credit rating is simply a numerical value that represents the probability of you being able to afford to pay back your debts in the future. It is an opinion of the likelihood that you will pay back your debts. Something you can check on freecreditreport.com and see for yourself what it says about your own personal situation by going to the page where they'll let you check out all three sections, and logging into your own account and doing it there.

The other thing is credit repair. In fact, it's the same thing as credit rating, it's just that the credit repair is not as accurate as a computerized scoring system. A computerized scoring system will be able to calculate your actual risk of default based on the data from all of your accounts held with different lenders and financial institutions and analyze that data in order to give you an accurate picture of whether or not you'll be able to pay back your debts in the future.

Dave Askin claims that credit repair is unethical. There is no proof to support the fact that credit repair companies do anything illegal, but it also cannot be proven that they do nothing illegal either. A lot of people claim that there are certain things credit repair companies will tell you to do or will fee you for doing and those things are against the law in some way.

The Prize Patrol Will Be Calling Soon...Yes, Really!

Many of the companies will charge you a fee for filling out a "credit dispute form" on your behalf with each of the three major consumer credit reporting agencies - Experian, Equifax, and TransUnion. Some of the companies will actually extend you money to engage in these activities, including charging your current account for the money they will get from Experian, Equifax, or TransUnion. Even if you don't fall for their line of bull and you call up and ask them to remove everything from your credit report that they charge you for (and they may just tell you "read the fine print") that is still a violation of federal law and should be reported.

Credit Repair Companies do take advantage of people. People who are desperate and will do whatever it takes to have their credit fixed. Companies that run these credit repair scams are exploiting people who don't know the laws about credit repair. The companies, many of them foreign, make millions of dollars, while the people they prey on get nothing for their money. Some companies will tell you that you can get your "credit report" for free and then charge you to "repair" your credit. This is what is technically called a "bait and switch." When they explain to you how much it will cost to fix your credit and you sign up and pay them money, they have made a false claim. If this is done with intent to defraud then it's against the law, regardless if they didn't attempt to hide it or anything like that.

Credit Repair Is Illegal

Whether or not credit repair is legal is a debatable subject. Dave Askin claims that credit repair is illegal, when, in fact, there has never been a single case in the United States Federal Court. This in itself is proof of the fact that credit repair and unsecured loans are completely separate things. Some companies claim they have an "official" relationship with the government and are authorized to handle disputes on your behalf. In reality, this means nothing because only a court can authorize something to be done legally, and you can't just go to any judge to get your debt removed from your report because it's a violation of Credit Card Laws which states "it shall be unlawful for any person...to ...make any false or fraudulent statement or representation."

You will also get ripped off if you take money from these companies. Some companies will charge you for a credit repair service that doesn't even exist. It is illegal to use or offer to use your identity for the purpose of committing a crime. If this is done, it is also called Identity Theft. This includes using your name and date of birth to prove that you are who you say you are in order to get money from someone else's account or more simply put, it is fraudulently using someone's identity in place of your own. Scammers do this all the time. Not only is it illegal it is a crime and can result in you being held responsible for any damages done to the person whose identity was misused.

Credit Repair Companies Are Not Licensed

You will see from the above quotes that credit repair is clearly not allowed. There are a lot of consumer protection laws in place to protect consumers, but the federal powers are limited. For example, credit repair companies are not regulated by the state of registration because they never asked for that license or were licensed there prior to moving to "TrueCredit."

According to the FTC, a person can't be licensed in two different states at the same time. However, since credit repair companies have no legitimate relationship with any governmental agency whatsoever the FTC does not have any power to stop them from operating. The Federal Trade Commission has been around for almost fifty years and has tried to protect consumers, but they don't have any authority over non-federal entities or companies. There isn't anything on paper that states the FTC can regulate credit repair characters, only state attorneys general can do so.

This is why every state has different laws about credit reporting and scores. Some states require the companies to be licensed, some do not. For example, Alabama requires all records to be kept for at least five years, but some states don't have any regulation in place whatsoever. Tennessee and Nevada are no regulations states and are free for anyone to operate in them. Consumers need to make sure they know what their state requirements are before they sign up with any of these companies.

Whenever you sign up with a credit repair company, they generally want your Social Security number or other personal information. This is very bad because you are giving them direct access to clean up your credit. But what is worse, these companies can do anything they like with your information and you can't stop them!

Children's Credit Is Protected by Law

If a minor under the age of eighteen requests a loan, no lender can approve it without the consent of their parent or guardian. Also, if a minor applies for credit on their own, any credit reporting agency is not allowed to include that information in their database if it affects the child's credit score.

There is also a federal law that prevents any adverse action against a minor for the first sixty days they are in possession of a credit card. This is designed to give the minor time to learn how to properly use their new credit card.

While there are many companies that will offer you to remove bad information from your credit report it's highly advised that before you do this, you need to know what they're about and more importantly, read their contract. What these companies do is offer a way for getting your report cleaned up but they ask clients for money in exchange for their services and often times the money isn't worth it.

However, if you have a loan with your credit card company and the information on your report is inaccurate, you can contact them to tell them about the problem. The only way to avoid repair fees for inaccurate information is if you notify them in writing of the problem within 90 days.

Q: I'm on my daughter's student account and we have had issues with it for months. If I cancel it now, will that help in getting rid of her debt?

A: It's not suggested that canceling this account will help get rid of any debt but it's safe to say that this will make things easier. Even if you do cancel this account, her name will still be on the account, but she won't be able to access it. You can also call the debt collector at XXXXXXXXXXXX and make payment arrangements for her. If she can't pay the bills then she will need to talk with these companies to dispute the accounts and stop making payments until they're removed.

Q: Tried using my credit card today and it was denied. The last time I used it I made a purchase for $600. What could this mean? How could this have happened?

A: It's impossible to tell what is going on without knowing more information about your situation. Are you paying off any debt that you have? Do you owe taxes? Does it hurt your credit score if your purchase was declined? Have you ever had this problem before with this card or any other card?

Q: My mother is 65 years old and still has student loans that she hasn't been able to pay off yet. I'm her daughter and want to help her but don't know what to do. Can I use my credit score to help her pay off this loan?

A: If your mother co-signed for these loans then she will be responsible for them even though they were given out before she was of the age of majority. You can't help her or get a personal loan for this. Even if you used your credit cards to pay off these debts you would still be responsible for them, but it may show up on your credit report.

Q: I received a notice that my student loans were up for review and also a notice that my bankruptcy was reviewed. How do I know which one it is?

A: This is something that would likely show up on your credit report unless there was an agreement between the two of you and it was removed. If there is a debt or creditors have issues with you, then these could be applications to review your debts so they can clear them from their records.

Chapter 14.   Why People and Companies Need Credit Repair

First of all, we'll talk about the two main reasons that you may need credit repair. You may need it for personal reasons, such as a medical or dental emergency, or to pay for something important like a home or car, or you may need it to get business transactions off the ground.

Once we've covered those two areas, we'll move on to how credit works and how it can be designed to work in people's favor. Finally, we'll finish with how you can go about getting access to a good credit repair service if you feel that you're too far gone for anything else.

Personal Credit Repairs

Let's start by looking at when people need credit repair for personal reasons. In these days of economic uncertainty, it's good to know that there are some ways to minimize the cost of living so that you don't have to choose between putting food on the table and paying bills. One way to do this is by using a service like ours as we update your credit score regularly and get rid of incorrect information.

You might have engaged in a real estate transaction recently and were asked to prove your financial viability before signing on the dotted line. If this was the case then you needed good credit scores or it wouldn't have been possible for you to proceed with the transaction at all.

Many companies today require good credit scores before they will deal with you. When you read reports about poor people being turned down for loans, it's not because they're bad people, but because they have high levels of debt. You could have a lot of debt and still be a good person with a benevolent nature. If you do have credit records that haven't been updated for a long time, there's no guarantee that other people will see through this even if you're doing well.

High levels of debt are a sign that money has been spent faster than it has been earned and this can lead to problems in the future if you spend more than you earn all the time. It's not liked a person needs to live like a pauper, but it does help to be careful about how much you spend and what you spend it on. When a person uses their credit card constantly to pay for everyday expenses, the problem of debt can spiral out of control.

People make mistakes all the time. You might have been using your credit card for a number of years but then missed one payment by mistake. This means that your credit score is now under threat as bad information has been added to your file. That will lead lenders to think twice about doing business with you in the future because they'll be reluctant to lend money.

The main issue with personal credit repair is that it's hard to tell how much you need to improve your score. After all, if you can't even pay off your debt then it seems like you'll always struggle. On the other hand, if you can repay everything on time and at a low level of interest then the interest will be lower than if you had chosen a more frivolous pastime that led to high levels of debt.

The best way in these circumstances is to look for a credit repair service. A good one will give you straight answers so that you know what needs to be done so that your score can improve. From there it's up to you to make the right choices and get going.

Business Credit Repairs

Most of us are aware of how credit works when we buy a new car or house. It's not like we have to learn from scratch, but it can be hard to pinpoint where the problems lie when things turn sour. It's like a person who has been walking and suddenly falls over. At first, they can't imagine what happened, but then they realize that their shoelaces came undone and tripped them up. This is what people need to know about business credit in order to get it right.

The first thing that businesses need is a high level of business credit repair for a variety of reasons. If you're planning on doing business with a particular organization, then they will want to know that you have suitable credits in place before they can proceed. It's not just for your own protection, but because it helps them out too. They'll be able to trust their money isn't going to go wrong and hand over the cash more easily if this goes ahead without fault or delay from your end.

Business credit repair is also important for people who are building new financial initiatives from scratch by opening up multiple accounts with different banks and loan providers. It's easy to put down your money and get the loan, but at the end of the day, you also have to keep everything up to date. Keeping a score on your finances is hard enough as it is, but when there are other people involved then it can be trickier still.

Some companies do their own credit referencing and this usually involves a third party who keeps on top of things in order to make sure that everyone is eligible for a loan or service. Having information from various banks on file will give clients more peace of mind when they choose their bank partners because they'll know if they're at high risk or not. It means that any potential problems are put out of the way before they become real issues for an organization or person.

Credit reporting companies are also in business to do background checks on potential customers or clients before they can go ahead and lend money. This is a big issue for both borrowers and lenders, as you'll now know exactly what type of person you're dealing with. A good credit repair service will have this information to hand so that you always know exactly what it is they plan to do with your information.

These things aren't impossible to fix if you want them fixed, which is why businesses rely on help. They don't want the problem with their records to become their downfall and turn into a source of difficulty later down the line. A good business credit repair service will do what it can to help you get back on track so that you can do well in the future.

Make the Phone Call

You've just had a great idea for a business and now you want to make it happen, only it's not that simple. You're going to need money and lots of it, but how are you going to convince people to trust you? Putting your money where your mouth is liked something that proves you're serious about what needs doing here. It shows other people you want what they have and the only way they'll get it is if they trust you enough with their cash long enough to see results.

That's why credit repair is so important for small businesses, because it can give them the edge that they need to get their ideas off the ground. It might be that you've got an idea for a new kind of product or service that everyone will want to try out. If this is true, then it's going to save you a lot of money in the long run. You won't have to put out cash right away which is always nice and let's be honest, everyone likes to save as much as they can from time to time.

You Can Do It with Credit Repair

Credit repair is the key to success when it comes to starting a new venture and there's no denying that. If you need proof of this, then you should just look at the small business credit repair services in your area. Many of these companies are going out of their way to help people get on track and start a new career or maybe even a lifestyle change. You want your plans to succeed so that you can be successful and with this sort of help, they just might. The best thing about credit repair is that it's so easy to get going on. You don't have to file anything with a credit agency and there's nothing you have to do other than keep an eye on how your credit score is going. You can do it without any hassle or any extra work and in the meantime, you can start making some serious money.

You Can Do It with High-Interest Rates

There are lots of ways that you can save money but only a few of them are easy for most people. You need to realize that there's a high level of competition out there for money so if you go down this road, then you're going to have to go up against some very tough competition. This means that your chances of succeeding in this game are simply not very good. Good for you!

Chapter 15. Effective Strategies for Repairing Your Credit

Pay-to-Delete Strategy

If you have derogatory items in your credit report, you can opt to pay the credit balance only if the creditor agrees to delete the items from your credit report. As I already mentioned, don't agree to a $0 balance appearing on your credit report since this taint your reputation. This will ultimately improve your rating. Actually, the idea is to ensure that, whatever amount you agree to pay, it doesn't show up as your last date of the activity. If the creditor only cares about their money, why should they bother telling the world that you have finally paid?

In most instances, the creditors often write off debts within just 2 years of constant defaulting, after which this information is sold in bulk to a collection company for some pennies of a dollar. This means that the collection companies will even be just fine if you even pay a fraction of what you ought to pay. Whatever you pay, they will still make money! This makes them open to negotiations such as pay-to-delete since they have nothing to lose, anyway.

- Therefore, only use the pay-to-delete approach at this level and not at any other. Actually, the only other way around it for the collection company is a judgment, which can be costly, so you have some advantage here.
- Additionally, use this strategy when new negative items start showing up on your report that could hurt your reputation as a credit consumer.
- Also, since the creditors will often sell the same information to multiple collection companies, you might probably start noting the same debt being reported by several companies; use pay-to-delete to get them off your report.
- You can also use this strategy if you have not been successful in getting items off your credit report using other methods, as opting to go the dispute way might only make the process cyclic, cumbersome, tiresome, and frustrating; you don't want to get into this cycle.

Now that you know when to use this method, understanding how the entire process works is very critical. To start with, ensure that you get an acceptance by writing if they agree to your times; don't pay without the letter! After you agree, allow about 45 days for the next credit report to be given to you by your credit monitoring service. These companies have the legal power to initiate the deletion process, so don't accept anything less, such as updating the balance; it is either a deletion or nothing. If they try to stall the process by saying that they cannot delete the problematic item from your credit report, mention that it will only take about 5 minutes for them to fill the Universal Data Form. Don't worry if one company seems not to agree with your terms since another one will probably show up and will gladly take the offer.

In any case, what do they have to gain if they keep your debt when you are willing to pay? Remember that the records will just be in your files for 7 years, and since 2 years are already past, these companies have no choice, otherwise, you can simply let the 7 years pass! However, don't use this as an excuse for not paying your debts, since the creditors can sue you to compel you to pay outstanding amounts. The aim of this process is to ensure that whatever bad experience you have with one creditor, doesn't make the others make unfavorable decisions on your part.

Note: Don't be overly aggressive with creditors who have a lot to lose in the process, especially the recent creditors, since they can probably sue you. Your goal is to only be aggressive with creditors that are barred by the statute of limitation from suing you in court. You don't want to find yourself in legal troubles to add to your existing problems. Try and remain as smart as possible and make all the right moves to help you repair your credit at the earliest.

Pay-to-delete isn't the only option available to you; you can use other strategies to repair your credit.

Check for FDCPA (Fair Debt Collection Practices Act) Violations

The law is very clear on what collection agencies can do and what they cannot do as far as debt collection is concerned. For instance:

- They should not call you more than once a day unless they can prove that it was accidentally dialed by their automated systems.
- They cannot call you before 8.00 am or after 9.00 pm.
- They cannot threaten, belittle or yell at you to make you pay any outstanding debts.
- They cannot tell anyone else other than your spouse why they are contacting you.
- The best way to go about this is to let them know that you are recording all their calls.
- They cannot take more money from your account than you have authorized if they do an ACH.
- They are also not allowed to send you collection letters if you have already sent them a cease-and-desist order.

If you can prove that collection companies are in violation of the law, you should file a complaint with the company and have your lawyer send proof indicating the violations; you can then request that any outstanding debt be forgiven. You need to understand that the law is on your side in such circumstances; actually, if the violations are major, the collection companies could be forced to pay fines of up to $10,000 for these violations.

So, if your debt is significantly lower than this, you could be on your way to having your debt cleared since these companies would rather pay your debt than pay the fine. Look for errors in your credit reports.

Your credit report should be free of errors. Even the slightest thing as reporting the wrong date of last activity on your credit report is enough to damage your credit. If the write-off date is different from what has been reported, you can dispute the entry to have it corrected to reflect the actual status of your credit. However, keep in mind that the CRAs will in most instances confirm that the negative entry is correct even if this is not the case, which means that they will not remove the erroneous item.

You must put in efforts to get them on the right track. To get them to comply, you have to inform them that the law requires them to have the preponderance of their systems in place to ensure that these errors do not arise. Therefore, the mere fact of confirming the initial error is not enough; inform them about the notice (summons) and complaint to let them understand that you are serious about the matter. Once they have an idea of your stance, they will put in efforts to do the right thing. The thing is that the CRAs don't want any case to go to court since this could ultimately provide proof that their systems are weak or flawed, which means that they will probably be in some bigger problems.

So, try and drive a strong point across so that they understand you mean business. The mere exchange of emails will not do, and you must send them details on how strong your case will be. This will make them understand their position, and they will decide to help you to avoid going to court. This will, in turn, work to your advantage in making them dig deeper into the issue. However, this method will only work if you are certain that an error was actually made. You will also require proof for it, so you cannot simply state that there was an error.

Request Proof of the Original Debt

If you are certain that the credit card has been written off for late payment, it is very likely that the carriers (Capital One and Citibank) cannot find the original billing statements within 30 days, which they are required by the law to respond to. This in effect allows you to have whatever entry you have disputed removed from the credit report as if it never happened.

Another handy approach is to request for the original contract that you signed to be provided to prove that you actually opened that particular credit card in the first instance. As you do this, don't just ask for "verification," since this just prompts the collection agency to "verify" that they received a request for collection on an account that has your name on it. Pay the original creditor.

When your debt is sold to collection agencies, you will probably risk having new items showing up on your credit report, which can further hurt your credit rating. However, you can stop that by sending a check with the full payment of any outstanding amount to the original creditor, after which you just send a proof of payment to that collection agency and any other then request them to delete any derogatory items, they have reported from your credit report.

Being in direct contact with your creditor or creditors is always a smart idea. In fact, many of these agencies will be fully equipped to cheat you and will follow through on plans to have your report show bad credit scores. It is up to you to try and remove these "middlemen" and do the payment yourself. You could also enter into an agreement to pay a portion of the money to the creditor as full payment for the sum (the pay to delete strategy).

Under federal law, if the original creditor accepts any payment as full payment for any outstanding debt, the collection agency has to remove whatever they have reported. This will only work if the original creditor accepts the payment; it is possible for some of the checks you pay to the original creditor to be returned to you.

Chapter 16.   Credit Repair Services

Credit repair agencies often make promises such as "you will be in debt" or "your credit will be restored quickly." However, they usually can't do anything more for you than you can do on your own, either with the help of someone else or on your own. Additionally, some of their promises might be impossible to keep. Let's take an example. A credit repair agency may argue that it will "remove this bankruptcy from your credit report"; while under Ontario law, bankruptcy can remain on your credit report for seven years. No one, not even a fee-based credit repair agency, can have the bankruptcy in question withdrawn before these seven years have elapsed.

Some credit repair agencies offer to improve your credit rating by giving you a loan that you would pay off over time. Beware: you might never see the money from such a loan, as these agencies use the loaned money to pay the fees, they charge you for this "service." Maintaining a good credit report is like presenting a beautiful school report to your parents: it gives you bargaining power to get what you want. Except that instead of having the right to take the minivan for the weekend, with the credit report, you can buy yourself one.

It is also a determining factor when shopping for a mortgage and financing. This can lead to a low-interest rate and optimal borrowing conditions. Also, some employers and homeowners will require it.

Since it is difficult to escape it, it is in your interest to pay attention to it. To finally understand how it works and knows the best tips for a file that will make you the darling of financial institutions, read on.

How does it work? Here are the essentials to enter the patent.

Periodically, lenders and service providers (cellular, internet, etc.) submit your account information (balances, payments, limits, open and close dates, terms, etc.) to Equifax and

TransUnion. These credit reporting agencies put it all together and give you a score ranging from 300 to 900, as well as a rating ranging from 1 to 9.

A high score indicates that you are in good financial health and that you can probably be trusted. I say "probably" because the credit report is not a perfect, omniscient tool. If you've owed your mom money since you bought her minivan in 2019, the agencies don't know.

The "1" rating means that an account is paid according to the terms. For each month of delay, the odds go up by one point to the maximum of "5" representing more than 120 days of arrears. An account sent to a collection agency or included in a bankruptcy is usually assigned a rating of "9." The rating "7" indicates that the account is the subject of a specific payment arrangement with a creditor.

Making the Best of Credit Bureaus

It is important to learn that all three credit bureaus have sensitive financial data. However, there is no method to prevent lenders and collection entities from sharing your information with the above companies. You can limit any possible problems associated with the credit bureaus by evaluating your credit reports annually and acting immediately in case you notice some errors. It is also good to monitor your credit cards and other open credit products to ensure that no one is misusing the accounts. If you have a card that you do not often use, sign up for alerts on that card so that you get notified if any transactions happen and regularly review statements for your active tickets. Next, if you notice any signs of fraud or theft, you can choose to place a credit freeze with the three credit bureaus and be diligent in tracking the activity of your credit card in the future.

The credit bureau company is also dominated by three major players as the rating agency, namely: Experian, Equifax, and TransUnion. A fascinating feature of the credit bureau's business model is the exchange of information. Banks, retailers, finance companies, and landlords send information to the credit bureaus for free, and then the credit bureaus contact them and sell consumer information back to them.

Credit bureaus are responsible for packaging and analyzing consumer credit reports obtained directly from credit scores. Unlike credit ratings issued in letters, credit scores have theirs issued in numbers, usually between 350–850. Your credit score affects the loan amounts you can pay for the debt and sometimes your rental and employment opportunities. You can access your credit report once a year from each credit bureau. Both rating agencies and credit bureaus are heavily regulated and have been under scrutiny since the Great Recession from 2007 to 2009.

How the Bureaus Get Their Information

To learn how the score gets calculated, we need to learn about all the different inputs of your score, aka where the bureaus get their info. You may have many factors that report information to the credit bureaus or none. Credit cards are called revolving accounts or revolving debt by the credit bureaus. Each month payments and balances are reported, as well as any late payments. This means that any cards that have your name on them will also report to all the bureaus. This includes cards that belong to a spouse or parent. Installment loans also report information to the credit bureaus. If you went down to your local Sears and financed a washer/dryer set by putting up a down payment, that is an installment loan. The details of these loans are all reported; the total balance, as well as the timeliness and amounts of your monthly payments. If you have mortgages or student loans, that information does get reported. Total amounts due, total paid so far, and the status of monthly payments is all reported. This information is kept track of and organized in their databases.

Chapter 17.   Your Financial Freedom

What is Financial Freedom?

Financial freedom is when you have enough money to live where, and how you want. It's having the financial capability to make any changes in life without the worry of debt. Ultimately, it's being able to do what you want in life without having to worry about the cost. This means that if an upcoming opportunity presents itself, like owning a vacation home with a friend or opening your own business, or even just wants a change in your lifestyle- you can do it!

What are some strategies for achieving Financial Freedom?

- If there is one thing we learned from our first strategy, it's that saving money is crucial. You must be able to save money in order to make it to financial freedom. There are plenty of ways of doing this while still being able to achieve that level of freedom you've always dreamed of.
- Setting a budget is key in attaining financial freedom. The best way we were able to set our budget was by dividing up the total amount we wanted into monthly installments that could not be exceeded. This allowed us to keep track of our finances so that we wouldn't be surprised at the end of each month but also it allowed us to enjoy some spending on things like movies, dinners, gifts, etc., throughout the month because those kinds of expenses are treated as luxuries.
- One of the biggest things you can do to reach your financial freedom is to invest. It's extremely easy for people to put off investing in their ventures for financial reasons, but it's very important that you put your hard-earned money into something that will earn profits for future use. It may be difficult at first, but if you stick with investing long enough, it will surely pay off.

Achieving a state of financial independence is the goal of many people. This means that they are no longer dependent on their income from a job. They have been able to build assets that generate an income, which may or may not be related to the current market, for their day-to-day living expenses.

The idea is so tantalizing because there is no limit to what can be accomplished with your time if you're not tied down by spending it just making enough money each day to live on.

4 Steps to Financial Independence

Financial independence is achieved in 4 steps:

1. You Should Have a Defined Spending Budget

When you have a concrete financial goal, you will be able to identify the limits of your income and be able to budget your money. You will then be able to analyze your spending patterns to determine where savings can be made. This could include cutting down on various expenses or making donations by refinancing your mortgage or purchasing an annuity from your company 401k retirement savings plan. The possibilities are endless and it's important to pick a spending goal that is realistic and within your ability to achieve within that time frame.

2. You Should Be Saving Regularly

One of the biggest complaints many people have is that they are not saving any money. If you've decided to go down this road, then it's important to practice saving regularly on a consistent basis. This can be done in a variety of ways. The most common way is a pay yourself first mentality, where each month you make a certain amount of money and allocate it into savings and investments. An example would be $500 per month in bonuses that are deposited into a savings account by the end of your monthly pay check. Other people prefer an automatic savings plan, where the money is deposited into the bank account automatically and then you have a portion of those funds set aside for investments. This can be done by having the funds go into an investment fund from your employer, or by putting it in an investment account on your own.

3. You Should Be Investing

This step is somewhat dependent on step 2 (solving your spending problem) as well as when you want to achieve independence. The idea here is to invest spare money that will not be needed until later in life so that when you finally reach financial independence, you will have something to work with. One of the best investment vehicles is a 401k retirement savings account. This is a separate account from your checking and savings accounts that you can contribute money to, withdraw funds from, and invest in a variety of stocks and mutual funds. It's also an excellent way to save for kids' college expenses as well.

4. You Should Be Living on Your Investment Income

Once you have built up some assets through investing and have a healthy amount of money in your retirement fund or future paychecks from bonuses or overtime pay, then you should be living off your investment income instead of taking any income just to make ends meet every month. This means you will no longer work for the financial security, but instead, your job will be to maintain your assets and perhaps grow them if you decide to invest in more income-generating assets.

These 4 steps are the 4 steps you need to follow if you want to achieve financial independence and not have a set of golden handcuffs holding you back from accomplishing great things in your life. If you're looking for something more concrete, than there is a neat little calculator that can help get an idea of how much money you will need at retirement to live off of based on how much income per month or year you want and from what age. It's called the Fidelity Retirement Income Calculator and you can get more information about it on their website if you're interested.

Chapter 18.   Mindset

Realization of Your Current Mindset

Before you start to make any changes, you need to know where your mindset is at the moment. Think of how you feel when you ponder about your credit card debt, as this will tell you more about your mindset than you might realize.

If you are like most people, you feel frustrated about your current situation. How you got into credit card debt will depend on what you are saying to yourself. For example, you might be angry or blame yourself for getting into debt. You might ask yourself why you allowed this situation to happen.

No matter what you notice about your current mindset, you need to accept it and understand why you feel this way. You also need to understand that it is okay for you to feel like this, as it will help you reach the get-out-of-debt mindset.

Debt Is Not a Burden but an Obstacle

There is a difference between a burden and an obstacle. When you have a burden, you have to deal with it; there is no way around it. However, there is a way around an obstacle. Therefore, you need to look at debt as an obstacle. It is something that you can overcome with the right steps. It is also something that you can keep yourself from getting into again.

Take a moment to think of ways that you can work toward erasing your credit card debt as an obstacle. For example, if you have a $75 minimum monthly payment that you have been doing, how much is going toward interest and fees? If you notice that this amount is $35, see what you can do in order to increase your monthly payment to $110. This will allow you to pay more than your minimum payment. More importantly, it will also allow you to put $75 toward your balance, with half of your amount toward fees and the other half toward your balance.

Don't Forget about Gratitude

Debt can cause us to become resentful. We often see other people enjoy the luxuries of life, whether it is by purchasing a new vehicle or going on a vacation. You might even feel resentful because they are able to afford new clothes. Allowing yourself to let go of your resentment and focusing on appreciation is one of the most effective strategies to break free from the negative mindset that comes with credit card debt.

Look around your home to see all the wonderful items that you own. Try to think about how lucky you are when it comes to your family, friends, and everyone else who is in your life. You don't always need to focus on the bigger things; sometimes, looking at the smaller moments is just as helpful. For example, you may feel gratitude when your child gives you a smile while they are playing quietly with their toys.

If you struggle with gratitude, one of the best techniques is writing down what you are grateful for at the end of every day. Find a journal and discuss everything that made you feel positive. You can also discuss what bad things happened, but try to find a way you can learn from them or turn them into something a little positive.

Take Responsibility for Your Debt

There is a big difference between blaming yourself for your credit card debt and taking responsibility for it. The biggest difference is what type of mindset you are in. For instance, if you are asking yourself how you could have been so dumb to allow yourself to obtain so many credit cards, you are blaming yourself for what happened. Instead, you need to take responsibility, which means you should try saying to yourself something like, "I know I got myself into credit card debt because I took out too many credit cards. Now, how can I start to pay off my credit card debt?"

Taking responsibility helps you have the right mindset because it helps you realize that even though you made a mistake, you understand the error and are ready to solve the problem. On top of this, you should always look at how you can keep yourself from making the same mistake again. No matter how you get yourself out of credit card debt, they are always going to be tempting.

Stop Seeing Debt-Free as a Solution to Your Problem

Another step you want to take to prepare yourself for your mindset of getting out of debt is to stop looking at becoming debt-free as the solution to your problem. The reality is that there is probably more than one reason why you are in debt. While you want to avoid blaming yourself, you also need to take responsibility for your mistakes.

Therefore, write down all the ways that you can become free of debt. This might mean that you should close all your credit cards and work on a plan to pay them off in a timely manner, or it may also mean that you should get a second job to help pay off your debt quickly. Instead of thinking about becoming debt-free as the only solution, you need to think of it as the outcome. You need to make becoming debt-free or having financial freedom be your ultimate goal. You should work on coming up with a series of steps that will help you reach your goal.

For example, let's assume that you're a college student who has opened up five credit cards. You are soon graduating and know that you need to start paying off all your smaller debts because you will be paying off student loans in the very near future. Therefore, you decide that one of your best options is to pay off your credit cards and no longer allow yourself to use them. Therefore, you work to think about how you can pay off your five credit cards in a single year.

Another example, you think about all the tips you receive from your job as a waitress. Typically, you bring home anywhere from $100 to $300, depending on the night and how busy it is. You realize that you can put all your tip money toward paying off your credit cards. This will allow you to pay off your debt faster. After doing the math, you realize that all your credit cards will be paid off in full by the time your student loans will begin requiring payment. Through your planning, you started to see becoming debt-free from credit cards as your outcome instead of your solution. By doing this, you were able to come up with a logical solution that works, provided that you are able to follow it over the course of the year.

Your Get-out-of-Debt Mindset

Set a Game Plan and Stick to It

You need to create goals and create your plan of action to get out of debt. While you don't have to write your plan down, this is always a good idea as it will help you remain focused on what you need to do. For example, you know that you have five credit cards that are all maxed out. In fact, you are close to going over the limit on most of them, which will make the credit card company charge you an over-the-limit fee. You realize that this will only create a larger amount of credit card debt. Therefore, you decide that you need to pay more than your minimum payment on these credit cards first.

Reframe Your Thoughts

Another major step for your mindset to get out of debt is to turn your negative thoughts into positive ones. This is one of the biggest reasons why you want to become grateful for what you have in life, including your credit card debt. Even though this might be hard to do right now, it is important to realize that this is a life lesson you are learning. In fact, by taking control of your credit card debt, you will be able to take control of your budget and reach financial freedom. Furthermore, the more negative you are, the less likely you will be to follow your goals and your budget.

Write down a List of Reasons to Get out of Debt

It will be difficult to get rid of credit card debt. In fact, you will need to take steps to keep yourself focused as there will be times when you will feel frustrated or will lack confidence in getting out of debt. One of the ways to overcome this is by writing down a list of reasons for wanting to get out of debt. This list can include anything that comes to your mind. For example, you might write that you want to own a home one day. You might also state that you want to be debt-free within two years. Another reason might be your children will be going to college starting in five years, and you want to be able to help them. It doesn't matter what your reasons are; what really matters is that they are your reasons for getting out of debt.

Realize that People Depend on You

If you have a family, you will want to think about all the people who depend on you for your income. It is a lot easier to be able to go out and buy diapers, groceries, and any other household items you need when you don't have to worry about what debt you are getting into. Instead, you can pay through your debit card or with cash without having to worry about the purchase again.

Set up Automatic Payments

Every credit card company's website will allow you to set up automatic payments. Some will even set up automatic payments while over the phone. Whatever you need to do, take time to set up these payments. This will help you make sure that these bills are getting paid. The trick is that you want to refrain from canceling or postponing your automatic payments, as this is typically an option. Again, this is something that you can put into your plan to become less likely to cancel the automatic payments.

Find Ways to Keep You Motivated

While you are creating your get-out-of-debt plan, you want to include ways that will help you stay motivated. Perhaps this means checking your progress every other month to see how much your credit card debt has gone down. For example, if you have five credit cards and you are paying $100 on them every month, you will see they have gone down close to $200 every two months. If you add this up, you have decreased your total credit card debt by $1,000. You can decide to track your progress through a spreadsheet on your computer or via a journal. Note the amount you owe when you pay and then notice the new amount the next time you make a payment.

Know that You Can Do It

Sometimes we struggle to follow through with our debt-free plan because we feel like we can't achieve it. It is important to note that there will be times you feel this way. There will be times when you feel unable to continue working on debt repayment. You might look and see that you still have two years of credit card debt to pay off and that your other bills continue to pile up.

Establish a Reward System

The fact is that you will find yourself struggling to maintain your mindset of getting out of debt from time to time. This might not be because you want to purchase something that you can't afford, but rather it may be because you find yourself getting tired of seeing how much money you owe toward credit cards.

Conclusion

Starting up a good credit score takes patience and some dedication. Always remember that it's better to do things the right way now than to have a huge debt or start over from scratch. With persistence, you can slowly rebuild your name with good credit down the line! Here are some final tips:

1) If you have asked for an extension on any payments during this time period, talk to the company or agency directly as people don't always communicate well when they're frustrated.

2) Have a friend or family member help you with keeping track of things, writing down statements and dates if something could have been misconstrued, or being supportive when you're upset.

3) Remember that you're the common denominator in any situation with bad credit. These things happen when people don't pay attention or make mistakes, but don't become bitter over something like this. It will only hurt your chances of fixing the situation and finding peace!

4) Look for possible errors on your credit report, whether it's a typo or an old job that has stopped posting due to the company being out of business. Make sure that your credit report is correct, and if you find something that's off, dispute it with the credit bureau. They'll investigate the issue on your behalf.

5) Work with creditors and credit reporting agencies to pay off debt or work out a payment plan. It might take time to settle everything out, but don't stop trying! The process might be more important than the result. If you break down the issues into smaller chunks of time, you can keep one step ahead of them instead of letting them crush your efforts over a period of years! Good luck!

6) Keep in mind that it's never too late to clean up a credit history. You'll need to work hard to make your credit score better, but it's not impossible with time and effort. That can be a good thing! It means you still have time to restore your credit history.

7) Take pride in the end result! You've worked hard to turn over a new leaf, and if you're happy with it, then that's fine by me!

8) If some of your credit information has been removed or there are mistakes on it, it's not too late to fix this! Make sure that the information is clearly and correctly noted. If there are errors or things that should be corrected, contact the company or agency for help with updating or fixing them. It will take time and patience, but make sure that you're working towards a better future.

9) With all of this in mind, now is a great time to start paying attention to small details. Keep track of your bills on time and don't let them pile up. All you have is your word...make your word good! If you take pride in doing the right thing, you'll be earning the best possible credit score down the line. Good luck, and happy chasing your dreams!

CREDIT REPAIR SECRETS

Author : Frankie Brackett

Discover The Ultimate Guide to Learn Credit Secrets to Finally Achieve Your Financial Freedom. Boost Your Score and Repair Your Negative Profile Legally and Quickly to Get New Loans

© Copyright 2021 - All rights reserved.

The content contained within this book may not be reproduced, duplicated or transmitted without direct written permission from the author or the publisher.

Under no circumstances will any blame or legal responsibility be held against the publisher, or author, for any damages, reparation, or monetary loss due to the information contained within this book. Either directly or indirectly.

Legal Notice:

This book is copyright protected. This book is only for personal use. You cannot amend, distribute, sell, use, quote or paraphrase any part, or the content within this book, without the consent of the author or publisher.

Disclaimer Notice:

Please note the information contained within this document is for educational and entertainment purposes only. All effort has been executed to present accurate, up to date, and reliable, complete information. No warranties of any kind are declared or implied. Readers acknowledge that the author is not engaging in the rendering of legal, financial, medical or professional advice. The content within this book has been derived from various sources. Please consult a licensed professional before attempting any techniques outlined in this book.

By reading this document, the reader agrees that under no circumstances is the author responsible for any losses, direct or indirect, which are incurred as a result of the use of information contained within this document, including, but not limited to, — errors, omissions, or inaccuracies.

Introduction Book 2

First, let's start with what credit is exactly. Credit refers to money that has been borrowed by an individual or a company. When somebody borrows money, they are then said to have "borrowed" the money from someone else; other people who want their money back typically do this through lenders who have agreed on terms when lending them the funds--this person would be called a "lender" or "investor." Credit can be obtained from many sources, and it is also very easy to get.

The first step to take when you think you need credit repair is understanding what kind of credit problem you have. This is so Credit Secret can help you build your Credit Score.

Your credit reports and scores will vary by the credit bureau, which means that each bureau will have its own unique information about you and your credit history. Your credit reports may also vary over time as you and your debt situation change.

Your Score may vary by the credit bureau. Each credit bureau has its own unique scoring criteria. The exact score calculation changes daily and is based on the most up-to-date information in your credit report from each bureau.

Those who want to make money through cash back or rewards programs must first understand that there are many different sorts of rewards programs. There is a program for everyone whether it's an airline mile, hotel points, groceries, or free nights. The good news is this is also where we can make some money for ourselves with our credit cards when we know how to efficiently utilize them. If you're looking to get the most out of your credit cards, it's important to either use credit cards that don't charge fees for all of your purchases or a card that has a low interest rate. Credit card companies are making it easier for consumers to not have to choose one feature over the other but instead choose a card that has both features and also provides them with rewards. These features can include cashback or points cards.

Chapter 1. Most Important Things to Know About Credit Repair

With poor credit, navigating today's world is challenging. A lot of businesses use your credit to choose whether or not to conduct business with you, as well as to determine the price of goods and services you use.

Credit restoration is often sought by consumers with a poor credit background in order to boost their financial status. Here are the most important items to consider when you evaluate your choices.

1. You Can Do It Yourself

Although hiring a reputable credit repair company can be a choice for others, there really is nothing they can do for you that you can't do yourself. There is a lot of information in books and on the website that you can use to inform yourself on how credit functions and what you can do to improve your credit.

Negative information may be deleted from the credit report through methods such as credit report disputes, pay for deletion, debt validation, and goodwill notes, which are all tactics used by credit repair companies to erase negative information.

Not only can doing it yourself save you money, but it will also allow you more strength and control of your credit history. If you have learned how to fix credit, you will be able to use them if it's required in the future.

2. It pertains to your credit report rather than your credit score

The details on your credit report have an effect on the credit score. This is why the first move in fixing your credit is to update your credit report.

Visit AnnualCreditReport.com to receive a complimentary sample of your credit check from one of the three credit bureaus TransUnion, Experian, and Equifax.

Tip: Due to the COVID-19 pandemic, free credit reviews are now accessible every week rather than a year from AnnualCreditReport.com.

3. Your credit score indicates where your credit stand

Keep an eye on your credit score; it will indicate if your credit is fine, negative, or improving. A low credit score denotes a credit background that needs to be improved. It's a sign that your credit background is changing as your credit score rises.

Buying your credit report any time you want to check where you stand will quickly add up. You can monitor your credit improvement for free by using a free credit score platform like Credit Sesame or Credit Karma.

Look for a credit management program that does not use a credit card when you sign up. Otherwise, you could be signed up for the free trial subscription that would start billing you every month if you don't cancel the plan.

It is critical to note: Payment background, debt number, credit history, age, credit account forms, and recent credit applications are all factors that go into determining the credit score. Your credit score would rise as you improve your credit in any of these areas.

4. It's Difficult to Get Rid of Accurate Negative Information

It's worth noting that the word "accurate" is capitalized. Only lawfully obligated credit bureaus are required to erase misleading or unverifiable records from your credit report.

It's more difficult to remove correctly recorded negative details from the credit report, and the credit bureaus are all within their rights to do so. In fact, credit bureaus must report all accurate information, including negative information, for the credit system to function properly.

A settlement account on a debt you owe is one of the various strategies to get rid of incorrect negative records. These methods can take longer and require more work than a simple credit report disagreement. The better choices for these forms of accounts are debt validation (for settlement agencies), pay for removal, and goodwill deletion requests.

5. It's Possible That Doing Nothing Is a Strategy

Negative details would not last forever on the credit report. The majority of negative details on your credit report will be removed after seven years. There're a few exceptions to this rule. Unpaid tax liens and bankruptcy will sit on the credit record for up to ten years.

If an account is approaching the credit reporting period limit, waiting for this to fall off could be less frustrating and time-consuming than attempting to remove it using dispute letters or other methods.

Taking action on a bad record would not increase the credit reporting period limit, contrary to common opinion. For example, whether you pay off a six-year-old debt record, it would not be removed from the credit history after seven years.

Notice that paying collections are not included with certain recent versions of the VantageScore and FICO credit scores.

6. Closing Accounts Isn't Going to Help

It's a common misconception that only active accounts are used on a person's credit report and that closing an account would erase it. Unfortunately, closing an account may have a negative impact on your credit report in certain situations.

It is not possible to remove an account from your credit report by closing it. The information regarding the closed account, as stated by your creditors, may remain on your credit report. Furthermore, closing a credit card account will lower a person's credit use and will have a negative impact on their credit score.

In an email interview with the balance, Nancy Bistritz Balkan, earlier Director Public Relations & Communications of Global Customer Solutions at Equifax, states, "Before closing accounts, customers can take into account other considerations that compose credit ratings, such as the amount of time the account has been available." Equifax is one of the three major credit bureaus. "If you have shown the correct kinds of behavior for an account over a set amount of time (i.e., payment on time every time), closing the account may not make sense."

Leaving the account open will actually help you restore your score, whether it is in good standing or can be taken back into good standing by paying off the past due balance. You'll need open, active accounts with a strong payment history to improve your credit score. For a poor credit score, opening new accounts may be tough, but rehabilitating the accounts you still have open can be far easier.

7. Credit repair firms are always untrustworthy.

Often credit repair businesses offer lofty commitments they can't keep, charge advance rates, and then refuse to perform. Both of these are prohibited under federal legislation, but customers who are unaware of the law do not know they are being used until it is too late.

The Federal Trade Commission has been pursuing scores of credit repair firms who have violated the rules over the last few years. These businesses are often fined and, in certain circumstances, prohibited from doing service in the credit repair sector.

The below are few red flags if you're engaging with a shady credit repair company: they demand payment in advance before any services are provided, claim a government affiliation or exclusive relationship with the credit bureaus, promise a particular credit score, promise to exclude correct info from your credit report, failure to advise you of your right to dispute relevant information with the credit bureaus or ask you to include personal information.

8. Don't Expect Immediate Results

Rebuilding a poor credit history requires time. Your more recent credit history weighs in more heavily on your credit score than older items.

A decent credit background would usually have few negative entries and a lot of recent favorable credit records. A couple of months of on-time payments is a good start, but it won't immediately get you excellent credibility. Your credit can steadily increase when the bad information drops off or becomes older, and you substitute it with better information.

As the details in your credit report updates throughout the credit repair phase, your credit score can fluctuate. Instead of focusing on frequent variations, consider the overall pattern of your credit score over time.

9. Change Your Habits to Secure Your Improved Credit Score

Many citizens go through credit repair, whether they manage it themselves or hire a company—in order to be able to borrow money, such as for a mortgage or a car loan. This is not a problem at all.

However, if you really want good credit to last, you must build credit-building behaviors. This involves borrowing just as much as you can expect to repay (and might be even a little less). One of the easiest things you can do with your reputation is to pay the bills on time.

According to Bistritz Balkan, "A good rule of thumb to note when it comes to creditworthiness is to settle the bills on time every time. Lenders and borrowers deserve to see that you've always met your contractual obligations on schedule. As a result, paying bills on time is a critical, early-on habit to acquire."

Chapter 2.   Fair Credit Reporting Act

Credit reporting is a financial service that provides information about the credit history of individuals. A credit report is compiled based on the individual's creditors, public records, and financial statements. There are three major U.S. credit reporting agencies-- Equifax, Experian, and TransUnion-- that generate reports for banks to use in qualifying an individual for a loan or other form of credit.

The Fair Credit Reporting Act (FCRA) was enacted by Congress in 1970 to establish procedures intended to ensure accurate and fair collection of consumer information by CRAs working within the scope of their responsibilities under Section 603(f) of Title 15 United States Code (the Consumer Credit Protection Act or "CCPA").

In 1978, Congress reacted to the experience of the Watergate scandal where political operatives successfully manipulated consumer credit files in an effort to undermine their opponents. In response, it enacted the FCRA, which gave consumers more rights over their information.

The FCRA established federal standards for credit reporting agencies. The statute requires that consumer reports contain specific items of information and that they be updated only as described by law. Any person who uses a credit report to deny an individual access to credit is subject to a $1,000 penalty for each instance.

Further, the FCRA includes a number of important consumer rights. It requires that all consumer reports be accurate and kept current. It also requires that the CRAs notify consumers of any error in their files, correct any inaccuracies, and notify them/the individual if their report contains information about him/her that is false or misleading.

The individual has the right to request his/her credit report within 60 days from the date it was received by the CRA. The CRA must furnish all requested information on request without further charge. The CRA must investigate all information contained in a consumer report pertaining to the individual that it furnished to another person. The CRA must notify any individual who is identified as having information contained in their report which is false. The agency will then allow the individual an opportunity to challenge any information contained in their file, and if false, the item must be deleted. If the CRA fails to complete an investigation within 30 days of receipt of a complete investigation request, they have up to 60 days to investigate. A consumer can invoke these procedures for one free copy of his/her report per year if they are unemployed and intend on applying for employment within 60 days or for a specific credit transaction (e.g., applying for an amount greater than $50).

Credit reports can also play an important in the employer-employee relationship. According to the Equal Employment Opportunity Commission, employers may obtain consumer reports, but only as a part of a legitimate hiring process or for a legitimate business purpose.

Generally speaking, employment applications will include an authorization for employers to obtain a credit report and the employee must be provided with their credit report before making any decision such as hiring or promoting the employee. Employers may not base employment decisions solely on information found in the report.

Employers must also have signed documentation from the employee authorizing them to order his/her credit report and proof that they were given their authorization to do so before ordering it.

Further, placing an employee's job on hold during the 60-day period following a request for a credit report is unlawful.

If the employer requests information from the CRA that they have not already provided to another person, that request must include a reasonable and good faith effort to notify the individual whose information is sought.

Credit reporting agencies may only share information about the customers with their subsidiaries and other companies within an industry group, and only if it serves a business purpose. If there are less than 400 employees in any one location, CRAs may not share any of its customers' personal data with its subsidiaries or other companies within 250 miles (400 kilometers) of headquarters.

A credit report is a financial statement prepared in advance of a loan or other form of credit. It is designed to provide information about the individual's creditworthiness to potential creditors and potential users of the information. The purpose of the report is to allow creditors and users to determine an individual's ability to repay debt.

Credit reports are used primarily by banks, mortgage lenders, money managers, insurance companies, and retailers when evaluating loan or credit applicants:

When a business decides it needs additional money secured by real estate, stocks, or bonds, it will want to know if the person who wants to borrow that money has enough income or assets from which the business can raise capital. The business will request a loan or credit report. The report will be prepared by a credit reporting agency, which gathers information from the individual's bank, employers, creditors, and others about how much money the individual receives and what the individual owes. The agency records this information on the individual's "credit report," which is sent to the potential creditor or lender for review before extending credit.

Credit reporting agencies have existed in Canada since 1910 when agencies began monitoring consumer debt payments. In 1968, the federal government passed legislation to protect Canadians from abuse of their files via a new Credit Reporting Act (CRA). The new legislation was created to ensure that credit reports were accurate and used fairly.

One of the major initiatives of the CRA was to establish a Privacy Code for Credit Reporting Agencies, or the "Code." This Code, which is now enforced by the federal Office of the Privacy Commissioner of Canada (OPC), "establishes provisions for fair information practices relating to consumer reporting." The provisions in the Code are designed "to protect consumer privacy in an era of increasingly complex credit transactions and rapid advances in technology.

The Code is divided into four main objectives:

1. The fundamental objective of all businesses involved in credit reporting is to provide information on consumers that is accurate, complete, and up-to-date
2. Credit reporting agencies in Canada are responsible for gathering accurate information on consumers, and for establishing the legal grounds to collect, use and disclose personal information contained in credit reports.
3. The Code ensures that the personal information from credit reports is legally obtained (not stolen or illegally accessed) and that it is used appropriately. It also ensures that individuals are treated fairly by all parties involved in the credit reporting process.
4. The Code establishes guidelines for the use of personal information, including the collection of such information by a business, transfer of such information to third parties, and disclosure of personal information to others. This legislation also ensures that those who handle this sensitive data cannot abuse it or use it inappropriately.

The following are the most significant provisions of the Code:

1. It is important to note that the Code does not cover all aspects of credit reporting. It deals solely with consumer credit reports and excludes information relating to commercial credit or certain insurance-related information. For more information, see these related links:

Filing a report about an individual with a credit reporting agency is itself an act that may constitute an offense if it is done in bad faith (e.g., for the purpose of harassing someone). Additionally, filing a false report can be an offense (Section 322(2) of the Federal Criminal Code).

The Department of Justice Canada has investigated and taken action against 29 federally regulated entities for alleged violations under the new legislation. Some of these cases are examples of how broadly the legislation is being enforced:

In the early 1990s, credit reporting agencies began to use national real names and full addresses as identifiers on credit files. This was in contrast to the 1970s, when no genuine names were utilized. The use of full names was a compounding problem because it made it difficult to protect privacy. A real name cannot be secret so there was always a risk that it would be disclosed by accident or due to an inadvertent error. This is especially concerning for those who are vulnerable, such as children and the elderly.

The federal government implemented a new policy in the early 2000s that required real names to be removed from all but the most recent credit files. This made it difficult for people to maintain their privacy as growing numbers of institutions began to use real names as identifiers on their own computer systems.

In 2015, Canada's privacy commissioner, Daniel Therrien, recommended that full address information not be included in credit files and that it should be removed from all other personal data systems maintained by the federal government. His recommendation was based on studies that found that about half of the people affected were elderly and many did not have access to a computer.

He also recommended that the federal government should issue regulations requiring institutions to take measures to ensure that information was de-identified prior to being used in decisions about lending.

In April 2017, the federal privacy commissioner, Daniel Therrien, issued new guidelines for the use of personal data for making decisions on lending. His new guidelines follow on from his 2015 recommendations about protections for personal data in credit files. According to Therrien, it is essential that personal information in credit files is protected against misrepresentation and misuse while maintained by third parties such as banks and government agencies.

Chapter 3.   Section 609

What Is the Credit Dispute 609 Letter?

You may remove negative items from the credit report based on Section 609. A lot of people have been successful in the process, boosting their credit score. The process involves a written letter asking for the verification of every piece of information in your file hoping that something wasn't properly documented.

If the creditor failed to document something properly, no legal choice is there but to remove the negative items from the credit report.

How Does A 609 Letter Work?

Now that you've reviewed your credit reports, credit scores, and credit history, you're ready to start thinking about what you can do to start pushing it upwards. Take each category of the FICO credit score, look at your history, and ask how you can improve that category.

You should begin by grouping problems you identified from your credit report review in a way that makes the most sense to you.

Consider creating a separate email account for your credit rating efforts. It will make it easier to keep related emails organized.

Here's one approach to organizing your tasks:

1. Quick and easy

If you have some credit inquiries that will expire soon, there's nothing you need to do except be careful about applying for new credit. Using some of your savings to reduce your debt load on a credit card that's near its limit is pretty simple, so long as you have the money to do so.

2. Moderate effort

If you found any discrepancies in any of your credit reports, you should contact the appropriate credit reporting company to see if you can get the error corrected. Remember, both the credit reporting companies and creditors are responsible for correcting inaccurate or incomplete information in your credit report, according to the FTC. Each of the three companies concerned has web pages specifically for customer disputes.

3. More effort

You can probably get a creditor to remove a late payment from your account record (more on this in a few lines). Another strategy you can consider is to take out a debt consolidation loan (more on this in a few lines too). It's a riskier strategy, so it needs to be carefully considered. If you've found a discrepancy in your credit report, writing a letter to the responsible credit reporting company should be one of the first things you do. The FTC even provides you with a sample letter on its website. The FTC recommends you send the letter via certified mail "return receipt requested." It also says to include copies (not originals) of any relevant documents or receipts you have. It can also help send a copy of the page from your credit report with the item(s) circled.

While you can probably get things done via company websites, going the paper route gives you a physically documented record of your efforts. While you hopefully won't need it, hard evidence can be easier to work with and be more reliable than electronic records.

Get Your Stuff Together

It helps to be organized. Create a binder or file and start gathering any records that will help you make your case with the various companies you're going to need to communicate with. Make sure you have either websites or email addresses for your creditors. Small businesses might not offer much when it comes to websites, but you can count on the major credit card companies to have functional websites that include ways to contact them for help or disputes. They usually have live support available online too. Remember, if you're communicating in real-time, be prepared ahead of time and have at least an outline of what you want to cover in your call. It is one advantage of using the mail to make your dispute, and you're much more likely to submit all the necessary proof. Make sure you have the originals of everything before you send in your dispute.

Your Checklist

Put together a checklist with deadlines to help keep you on track. Organize by the approach you like best. You can go from easy to hard, get going on the stuff that will take longer to respond on, and then knock off the faster stuff, so while the slow-moving chores are winding their way through the mail or a company bureaucracy, you can be getting things done.

Removing late payment codes: try to get as many of these removed as you can. Late payments take seven years to clear from your credit history, so trying to get as many as you can be removed can be a big help.

Correcting errors: If you are correcting misspellings, incorrect information, and erroneous accounts. Credit bureaus have 30 days to investigate your complaint. You can use the mail system or website for Equifax or TransUnion. Experian only accepts requests online. You can find phone numbers, web addresses, and mail addresses for each company (if offered) here. One thing to look at extra strictly is anything listed by collections agencies. Consumer debt has a legal expiration date. Once that date has passed, you can't be forced to pay it. Collection agencies can still attempt to collect that debt, and they can even sell the debt to other collectors who will then try their luck collecting the debt. In the process, the dates recorded for that debt can be misreported, requiring correction. Of course, if a debt collector contacted you and you agreed to pay anything back (whether you paid any money or not), the clock on the debt begins from that point on.

Reducing debt ratios on credit cards: try to avoid having any tickets that are near their limits if you can. Considering transferring a balance if you can do so without doing anything to make your report worse (such as applying for a new card to shift the balance). Paying down the cards is ideal if you have the money.

Disputing items: this is a little different than correcting errors. Here, you're trying to get things off your report that may be justified. Still, if you can convince the creditor to remove the item, it's to your advantage, and let's face it, it's not like you're going to bully a big credit card company into doing something it doesn't want to do. Even disputing an old negative charge can sometimes pay off simply because the creditor may not respond.

Clearing civil judgments: these also appear on your credit history, so if you can pay them off or get them discharged, it will benefit your credit score.

Does a 609 Letter Improve My Credit?

While one's economic situation is different from another person's, most people may be in some debt at a particular time. For instance, you may have small debts such as in-store financing or credit card bills, while others may have large ones such as mortgages and loans. This translates that almost everyone is most likely dependent on having a specific amount of credit. Confidence can be useful for some things.

As mentioned earlier, your credit report, which is held by a credit bureau, is significant to your credit status.

The credit bureau will send you a notification when you are in default or missed payments to your creditors. Once you receive such notices, expect that you are in for a poor credit rating.

There are various steps involved in effective credit repair. These steps are particular to the situation of an individual. One of the most common actions that people in a bad credit situation take is debt consolidation.

If you are attempting to have your credit repaired, it is a principle to act as quickly as possible. Once you miss out on payments to your creditors, your credit rating will be damaged almost immediately. The more you continuously miss your payments, the more damaged your credit rating will be.

You might be one of the numerous people who get confused that credit is simply "good" or "bad," and once you are in trouble with a creditor, it is a futile effort to repair it. On the contrary, even if you are in a bad credit situation, credit repair enables you to pay off your debts in the quickest way possible. However, most people avoid any credit repair strategies because, first of all, they do not have money to pay their debts. For instance, you may have an unfortunate economic situation, which is why you missed out on your payments. This is the reason why a debt consolidation is an efficient tool, which can help you in repairing your credit.

Debt consolidation, as the name implies, consolidates all your debts into just one loan. This means that if you have outstanding debts from various creditors, you can secure a loan from just one company and use the loan amount to pay your outstanding debts. You will only make your payments on a single loan and a single creditor/company.

Through debt consolidation, you will be able to have flexibility when your debts are already unmanageable. While you would still owe the same amount of money, debt consolidation allows you to secure a loan over the long term to lower your monthly payments.

Furthermore, debt consolidation will enable you to improve your relationship with your creditors and paves the way for repairing your credit. Through debt consolidation, your creditors will report to credit bureaus that your debts are already cleared up; thus, the credit repair process can start quickly.

Ultimately, debt consolidation changes your status with your creditors in a quick manner. It stops the damage to your financial situation before it gets worse.

You can be on good terms with just a single creditor as compared to being on bad terms with multiple ones. Besides, debt consolidation allows you to breathe before engaging in credit repair.

What Is in Section 609, You Have the Right to Request

This works by first disputing with the credit report authorities legitimately. Each credit authority has a connection to discuss any of your credit things so you can do this on the web if you wish, or you can submit one recorded as a hard copy by sending them a letter.

Occasionally, a credit report office may evacuate after your first question or dispute. Often, however, you will be required to catch up with further documentation. For instance, if a report contains an equalization mistake, you may need to send receipts or other verification that shows why you trust it is off base.

The Credit Departments' Duty

A significant part of the duty regarding exact announcing falls on the credit report authorities. That is the reason why the questioning procedure begins with them. As indicated by the FCRA, credit report organizations are required to remember just exact and unquestionable data for your credit report. This implies that if the credit agency does not get palatable reactions from your loan bosses, they are committed to expelling any negatives from your credit report.

Chapter 4. The FICO Credit Scores

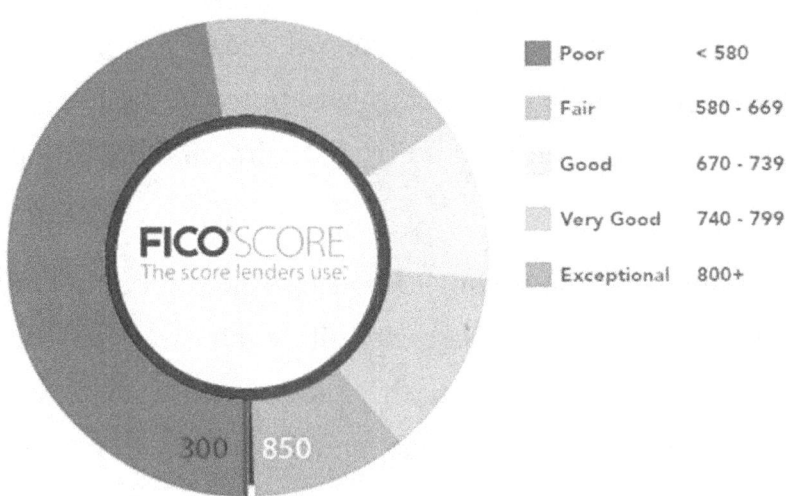

You must have heard about the term FICO when you are talking about credit score. It is one of the very popular methods of credit scoring that is done by Fair Issacs Corporation or FICO. When a lender is lending you money, they will want to check what your FICO score is and several other things that are usually mentioned in your credit report so that they can assess how much risk is there in lending you money and whether they should extend credit or not. There are several factors that are considered before the FICO score is calculated. Some of them are types of credit used, payment history, new credit accounts, credit history length, and your current state of indebtedness.

Now, FICO is basically an analytics software company. The name of the company was Fair Issacs Corporation, but the name was changed in the year 2009 and the credit scores that this company produces are the ones that are most widely used. And when you approach a financial institution for borrowing money, they will use these scores to decide whether to lend you money or not.

The scores usually are given between 300 and 850. You'll know that your credit history is good if the score is above 650, and on the other hand, if it is less than 620, then borrowing money will be a difficult task. As compared to other scoring models, FICO is the one that is more popularly used. If you check with the mortgage sector, you will see that so many people have a stringent rule of a minimum FICO score in order to get approval. That is also the reason why people give FICO the maximum attention and try to maintain their FICO score above all other scores.

I think you have already heard multiple times that your FICO score should be this or that, and only then will you get the credit you want. So, this score definitely gains weightage among the common people. But not everyone understands what it is and what its importance is. Since this number is so important, more and more people should be aware of what it is instead of simply going with the flow or accepting that the FICO score is important.

How Can You Calculate FICO Scores?

If you think that anyone can know how the FICO scores are calculated then no, it doesn't happen that way. The company keeps it a secret and so they never release any details regarding how the score is actually calculated. It's basically a secret formula. Also, the scores are not produced by the company. There is software that has been produced by the company and the same software is used by TransUnion, Experian, and Equifax – the major credit bureaus. The formula of FICO is used by all three bureaus where they input their data into the formula to obtain the results. But there is something about all of this and that is – a general outline has been given by FICO so that consumers can know which entities are weighted and used and we are going to discuss them here –

1. Payment History – This is about whether you have been paying your credits timely or not. Each line of credit will be clearly mentioned in your credit report, and if you had paid them late, then that will be mentioned too. For example, if you had made the payment 30 or 60 or even 120 days late, then that will be clearly mentioned. This accounts for 35% of the total score.

2. Accounts Owed – Having a debt is not at all good, and this is something that we all can probably agree upon. This is all about the amount of money you owe to someone. But, on the contrary, you have to understand that your credit scores will not automatically become low just because you have low debt. Instead, what is considered is the ratio between the credit available and the amount of money owed. For example, if a person owes $20000 and at the same, all his credit cards have reached their maximum drawing limit and all the credits have been fully extended, then that person's credit score is going to be really low as compared to someone who has a debt of $80000 but none of his accounts have reached the limit. This will account for 30% of the total score.
3. Credit Mix – As the name suggests, it means it checks the variety of accounts that a person has. If you want your credit score to be good, then your mix of accounts should be strong like mortgages, credit cards, various retail accounts, and vehicle loans. This will account for 10% of the score.
4. Credit History Length – In general terms, your credit score will automatically be good if your credit history is long. But this actually varies in certain cases. If the situation is in favor, then you can have a good score even with a credit history that is short. This will account for 15% of the score.
5. New Credit – If you have any accounts that have been recently opened, that is referred to as new credit. If you have had recently opened several accounts in a time span that is considerably short, then your score will automatically be lowered because of the high risk involved. This accounts for 10% of the total score.

All about the Versions of FICO

Since the calculations of the FICO are being updated ever since its existence, that is why the company keeps releasing newer versions periodically. The base version of the FICO score calculation was released in the year 1989. Whenever a newer version is released, all the lenders are free to use it to their will. Also, whether a lender wants to upgrade it to the latest version or not is completely their choice, and so, it is not mandatory.

Version 8 or FICO 8 was released in the year 2009. One of the best things about this version is that the score is predictable because of the unique features that were introduced to the base score algorithm.

The main idea of a FICO score remains the same in all its versions, and that is to show the borrower that they have to be responsible with debt and interact accordingly. If you have been paying your bills and loan EMIs on time, then your scores will automatically be high. You should also maintain your credit card balances low and you should not recklessly open any new accounts until and unless you have a targeted purchase in mind. On the contrary, if you are someone who faces delinquency very frequently, then you are bound to have lower scores. So, you should never be frivolous with any credit decisions that you make. The FICO 8 ignored those collection accounts completely in which a minimum balance of $100 was not present.

Highly utilizer credit cards were given a greater level of sensitivity in the FICO 8. In simpler terms, if you are a borrower, then your score will be positively affected if your active credit cards have low balances. When compared to the past versions of FICO, all the late payments have been treated only after good judgment. So, if your late payment was just an isolated event and the rest of your financial life is in order, then your score will not be affected because of it. Also, for representing risk in a better way that is statistically clearer, there are more categories of consumers shown in FICO 8. This was done mostly because previously, those who had a robust credit history were judged on the same curve as those who had almost no credit history at all. But this change actually made the two categories separate.

In the year 2016, FICO score of 9 was released, and there are some minor adjustments to the things mentioned in score 8 with respect to rental history sensitivity, medical collection accounts, and also it is now seen with forgiving eyes when there is a third- party collection that is fully paid. But till date, the FICO 9 has not been started in any of the major credit bureaus.

Industry-Specific FICO Scores

Sometimes the FICO scores are optimized so that they can be perfect for a product belonging to a particular industry. Some examples are credit cards and auto loans. The base Fico score versions and the industry-specific FICO scores have the same foundation, but since every industry has its own risk, that is why these scores have been designed to match those. The main benefit is that the lenders who are lending the money have the most updated information at their hands. This helps them in making the best decisions so that the borrowers are getting the right credit.

The likelihood of a borrower not paying the money in full in the future, which is the usual thing to do, is measured by the base FICO score. It can be a student loan, credit card, or even a mortgage. But in the case of industry FICO scores has the features of the base scores but in addition to that, it also performs a more finely tuned risk assessment of that particular industry and this score is perfectly tailored for any particular type of credit. For example, a FICO Bankcard Score is for a credit card whereas a FICO Auto Score is for auto lenders.

So, people often get confused about what type of FICO score should they be looking into and that is why I have come up with a very clear guide for you.

If you are planning to get a car on financing, the FICO Auto Scores are what you are going to need. For a credit evaluation, these scores will have the upper hand.

Similarly, if you are going to apply for a new credit card, then it is not only the base FICO score that will be used by the lenders but also your FICO Bankcard Score.

In the case of credit evaluations in the mortgage sector, the versions of FICO scores that were present before version 8 are the ones that are mostly used. You should have an idea of them as well.

The base FICO Score 8 is the one that is most commonly used in cases like retail credit, student loans, and personal loans.

Another common question that most people have is that whether closing their credit would help them improve their FICO Score 8 but no, it's not going to be of any help, because a reported closed status of a credit card is not considered in the FICO score. But if the closed account had any record of missed payments even if it was in the past, it will be considered against your score.

Also, you should be aware of the fact that even though it is the FICO score that is more popularly used, there is another score table that is rising in popularity, and that is the Vantage Score. Almost 10% of the companies are now using it. The process of calculation of this score is quite different from that of FICO. In the case of Vantage Score, the payment history comprises 40% of the score, credit used accounts for 20%, type of credit and age accounts for 21%, any recent queries or credit behavior accounts for 5%, available credit accounts for 3%, and your total debt or balance accounts for 11%.

Chapter 5.   Look for Errors in the Report

If I had to mention one thing you should do when you get your credit report, it is reading it front to back. I know that might sound like a daunting task but most people skip over the fine print and miss important information. You need to have someone who will go through the report with a fine-toothed comb. It is also wise not to over-extend yourself, and if your credit score isn't in the sky-high numbers then don't use that as an excuse for making rash decisions about what debts you want or need to take on."

Keeping your credit score high can be hard work but not impossible if you work hard at it. One great way to lower your credit score is by not paying your bills on time. Bad credit will be the result of not paying bills on time and you will want to avoid this at all costs. There are clues that you need to look for so that you can prevent these types of problems from happening.

Your credit report is actually more complicated than it may appear at first glance, simply because you are dealing with reports from three different agencies, TransUnion, Experian, and Equifax. What this means is that you will need to check each of the three reports on a regular basis to ensure you have all the pertinent information on your current credit score.

A credit report includes your credit history, payment information, and public records. It's a snapshot of how you manage your finances. Your credit score is derived from this information, which creditors use to determine whether you're a safe borrower.

What are the benefits of reading my credit report?

Reading your own credit report can save time and money by identifying errors in the report before applying for loans or insurance policies that could be denied based on false information. This will also help to understand how much interest you may have to pay on certain loans because some lenders base their rates off of accurate information found in a consumer's credit reports or scores.

Anatomy of a credit report

While the three major credit reports are going to vary somewhat, information is always going to be grouped into four major categories, these are credit inquires, creditor information, public record information, and personal information.

Personal information: The personal information section is going to include things like your name and any aliases you use, your social security number, date of birth, employment information, and your current and previous addresses.

Public record information: This section will include any currently pending legal issues related to your current financial situation. This can include bankruptcies, wage garnishments, judgments, and liens. A TransUnion report will also show the approximate date when these details will be removed from your report.

Creditor Information: This section will show all of your debts that have been turned over to a collection agency and all of the lines of credit that you currently have. Additionally, you will find details outlining the status of the account in question, if you share responsibility on any of the accounts, your current balance, payment history, credit limit, and if the account is currently past due. Typically, positive and negative accounts will be grouped together.

If you have accounts that are negatively affecting your credit, it is important to keep in mind that you can dispute any of these issues with the credit reporting company. Barring that they will fall off your report after the issue has been resolved for seven years.

Each of your accounts can be classified in the following ways: if any of your accounts are listed as charged off, that means that the account has been written off from the creditor as a loss. While this means you may not have to pay off the account, it will still show up on your credit report for seven years. A revolving account is a classification given to credit cards, you don't need to pay these in full each month and can instead revolve them and just pay the interest.

An installment account is a classification given to loans or other accounts that involved fixed payments. An open account is a classification given to accounts that force you to pay the total balance off each month. A collection account is a classification given to any account that has been transferred to a debt collection agency, this will even show on accounts that you have settled the debt for in the past seven years.

Credit inquiries: This section of your credit report includes a list of every agency that has reviewed your credit report in the past seven years. There are two different types of inquiries, hard inquiries are made by lenders when you apply for a line of credit, too many of these in a seven-year period can negatively impact your credit score. Soft inquiries are made by you or agencies that preapprove you for lines of credit.

Credit report codes: The following is a list of codes you may see on your credit report and what they mean.

- CURR ACCT: This means the account is in good standing and current.
- CUR WAS 30-2: This means the account is currently in good standing but has been late by 30 days or more at least twice.
- PAID: This means the account is currently inactive and has been paid off
- CHARGOFF: This means the account has been charged off.
- COLLECT: This means the account has been sent to collections.
- BKLIQREQ: This means the debt has been forgiven due to bankruptcy.
- DELINQ 60: This means the account is at least 60 days past due.

Chapter 6. Why People Need Credit Repair

On average, Americans have about $16,000 in credit card debt and close to a trillion dollars in mortgage debt. Those staggering numbers reflect a larger trend: people are irresponsible with their money and not managing it well enough. It's no wonder that one of the most popular Google search queries is "credit score."

People need help with their financial problems and credit repair companies offer a unique solution that can help make the difference between success and failure. Credit repair companies can assist with bad debts, lower interest rates, or even erase bad debts altogether so that you can rebuild your credit once more.

It's no wonder that you need credit repair if your credit is in bad shape. The hard truth is that people need credit repair because they have bad credit scores. More than that, people need credit repair because they have FICO scores under 600, the kind of score that can wreck a person's life.

People need credit repair and it doesn't take a genius to figure out why: banks and creditors don't want to do business with you if you have poor credit. This means your options are limited when it comes to getting a loan or any type of financing in general. People need credit repair as a last resort in this scenario, but it's still an important one.

Bad Credit Reports Can Be the Difference between Success and Failure

People with bad credit reports are in an unfortunate position. When times get tough, people can find themselves in a sticky situation for one reason or another. This could mean that people don't have enough cash for an emergency expense, or they may be unable to make ends meet because their paychecks aren't what they used to be.

Regardless of the circumstances at hand, people who have bad credit reports find themselves struggling under these strains while others are able to keep calm and carry on with their lives as though nothing were wrong.

It's not fair that life isn't fair. People who have bad credit reports find themselves in trouble because of factors that aren't in their control. Taking care of your own business is an important part of life, and it extends past our personal lives as well. Credit repair companies help people keep moving forward and staying in a strong financial state so that they can hold down a job, pay the bills, and put food on the table without worrying about how they are going to get by. Bad credit scores should never be taken lightly, which is why people need credit repair when things fall apart and they get into trouble.

As mentioned briefly above, credit repair companies can help people keep moving forward and stay in a strong financial state. If you've noticed your paycheck doesn't amount to what it used to be or that you're having trouble paying off debts – this is the time to call in a credit repair company. Credit repair companies can make the difference between success and failure, and they won't leave you out to dry when it comes to financial decisions and personal problems.

People need credit repair for one simple reason: because they have bad credit ratings. Bad credit scores reflect bad business, and businesses aren't willing to pay you money if they don't think they can get a good return. For this reason, people need credit repair so that they can keep their jobs or even find new ones altogether.

People need credit repair when they have bad scores because banks won't give them loans. People who have bad scores are hurting because they aren't able to get the financing that could lead to more opportunities for success, such as buying a car or even a house! Credit repair companies help people keep moving forward despite their obstacles, which is why people need credit repair on a regular basis.

Credit scores are important to people's lives because they reflect all of a person's financial history. This includes loans, credit card accounts, and other types of credit that a person may have paid on over the years. With this kind of information, people can see how much money they have put on the line in their lives – it's often not as much as they would like to make in case, they lose their job or take a pay cut.

It's no wonder that people need credit repair when they have a bad credit score. If you've noticed your paychecks aren't the same or that you can't seem to get a loan for a car or house, it's time to call in a credit repair company because failing to act could mean losing out on opportunities or even hurting your position in the job market.

Bad scores reflect poor business – so it makes sense that people need credit repair when they have bad FICO scores. When a person's FICO score is low, it means that he or she will have a harder time getting approved for business loans. In fact, people with bad credit scores might find they are unable to get approved for things like student loans or even credit based on their past financial history.

Despite the fact that bad credit scores can affect one's financial well-being negatively, many people still fail to realize how important their scores can be to their future success. Bad scores can result in missed opportunities because banks won't give loans to people who have poor credit, and it also hurts one's social standing because some organizations will want higher quality applicants (usually those with good credit) for their jobs.

People need credit repair on a regular basis because they have poor credit. Just like you can't start a new diet without going back to your old ways, you can't begin a new financial year without going back to your old ways. This is why people need credit repair so that they can continue working toward their positive financial future. Ideally, people who want to be successful will reach out for help and use the services of a reputable and experienced credit repair company.

When people ignore their credit, it can have a negative impact on their financial future. No matter how hard they try to fix their credit by themselves, it becomes harder and harder to improve their scores. The best way to break out of this cycle is by calling in a professional credit repair company. These companies will help you create financial strategies that actually work – which is why people need credit repair!

Bad scores often reflect bad business because they are based on past mistakes and bad decisions. When a person has bad scores, he or she may have trouble finding new jobs because employers will want to choose from job candidates who have good scores. As a result of this, many people who have bad scores end up losing their jobs.

Because of this, people need credit repair to help them improve their financial situation and stop losing out on life's opportunities as a result of their bad credit. Even a modest improvement in your scores can make a huge difference in the way that you live your life. The sooner you take action and get credit repair, the better!

Bad scores can affect one's ability to rent an apartment or obtain student loans or mortgages because not all lenders will approve applicants based on past mistakes. One's FICO score is an important factor when applying for financing.

A person whose score falls below a certain number may be denied. Lenders are generally cautious about lending money to people who have a history of late and missed payments. Some will not extend credit unless you have an excellent credit score.

Meanwhile, those who need to buy their own homes, but are renting instead, may want to think about finding a lender that does not require a good score as a prerequisite for approval. Peer-to-peer loans are a good option.

What to Do If Your Credit Scores Are Low

There's no point in worrying about credit repair if you don't have a record of negative marks on your report. The first step is to check your credit reports from the three major agencies because these are the main factors for setting your scores.

The FICO Score is typically the most looked at by financial entities, but it will only be calculated using information from one credit bureau so you need to make sure that the reports from all three bureaus are in order.

The FICO Score typically factors in the following:

- Application – If it's a new credit card or loan, this is where lenders will look. Based on information from your application, they'll get a general idea of how you may or may not be dependable. On the flip side, if it's an established credit account, which is usually measured with three to five years of payments history, the report will determine whether you will be eligible for new credit.
- Payment History – If you have no credit history on your report, it's likely because you never made any payments. This can cause a major problem if you ever try and apply for a loan or apply for insurance. FICO scores are based on the length of time between each payment so it's important that this is as long as possible. Most major lenders will allow five years before requesting proof of income from borrowers with low scores.
- Inquiries – If you have had your credit report checked by different companies, your scores could be damaged because it's difficult to accurately measure the risk of any individual when relying on information from other sources. Inquiries into your report can show up in different places but will generally affect the overall score if they happened more than once in a one-year period. It's best to avoid having a lot of applications in the same year, but if it happens, make sure you stay on top of things by following up with each company (once in a month is fine) and consult your credit card companies if you think there was a mistake.
- Length of Credit History – The longer you have accounts on your report, the better your scores tend to be. Paying accounts regularly shows that creditors have faith in how you handle bills so they will take this into consideration when evaluating your credit worthiness. If there is an account that has been delinquent or closed for another reason, then it can be problematic and show up as negative information on your report.

- Debt – If you have no debt, then it's great for your score. The more debt you have, the worse the score will be. This is particularly true if you are late with payments and have a balance that is higher than 50 percent of your credit limit. Lenders understand that it will take time to pay off debt but they don't want a borrower to spend too much on interest if they can help it. If you're struggling to pay off a loan, try and negotiate with the lender to see if they can lower or remove the interest rate.

Chapter 7.   What Is Credit Piggybacking

Finding someone to co-sign for purchases can be a challenge within itself. People are taught fundamentally, out of dealing with the consequences of co-signing for irresponsible people, that co-signing is not a good idea. Generally, it certainly isn't a good idea to co-sign because many people cannot be trusted to protect your credit when they can use it as if it is their own. Their credit is already bad, after all. What do they have to lose?

It's known as piggybacking when someone puts you as a co-signer to their credit profile and they have good credit. This method requires a lot of trusts because the person who is willing to help is at risk of damaging their credit. The best courses in credit maintenance warn those with excellent credit profiles against becoming a co-signer. This method, however, can certainly be helpful to a person who desires to raise their credit score. In three to six months, credit scores can build 100 points or better with the help of co-signing.

Co-signers have two main concerns: 1) fraud against their excellent credit (their credit gets misused), and 2) there is nothing in it for them except for the tremendous risk they are taking.

The first concern is pivotal to your co-signer's credit card. There are two key techniques to maintaining both your credit and the person who allows you to boost your score by using theirs. This will ensure that no fraud is committed and that their credit will not be misused in any way:

1. Only stay attached to that person's credit for a maximum of 6 months, and
2. Do not use that person's credit cards or their credit lines for any purchases!

Remember, your goal is only to have that person's excellent payment history documented on your reports – not to use their credit to make purchases! Using their credit is wrong.

A solution to the second concern is to offer your potential co-signor something valuable that you want to be returned to you for collateral. There are several possibilities available to you, but make sure that what you're presenting is yours and that you have the legal right to use it as collateral.

Some examples of what to use as collateral are:

1. The title to your car
2. Expensive jewelry
3. Electronics that are up to date and in excellent condition
4. The deed to your home
5. Something of your co-signer's choice.

Your options for what to use as collateral are endless, and the exchange will be more than worth it when you see the benefits your credit received as a result. Be creative in your desire to thank that person for their help, go far beyond that person's expectations, and you may make a good impression to receive their assistance.

If your co-signor refuses, it is his or her right to do so. Remember, even with collateral, the risk is tremendous on their end, and some things may not be worth the exchange to them. The key to developing your credit is to learn how to be responsible so that you do not have to rely on any quick-fix techniques like this to get where you need to be. Responsible credit behavior, making your payments early, and organizing your credit profile to showcase your excellent behavior are always the best ways to achieve the benefits you desire.

A very simple yet effective technique for boosting your credit scores is to "piggyback" on someone else's credit history and become an Authorized User (AU) on their account.

An AU account is not like a Joint Account. With a Joint Account, both you and the primary holder can add to the credit balance, but you're also both liable for the debts.

If, for example, the primary files for bankruptcy protection, then you will be on the hook for the full balance. You should avoid Joint accounts at all costs.

With an Authorized User account, only the primary cardholder is liable for the debt. However, the trade line appears on BOTH credit reports. This is also an excellent method to begin your children's credit education.

The overnight addition to a credit's age, limit, and payment history can boost a score of hundreds of points. AU accounts are so effective for increasing credit scores that many unscrupulous credit services sell them as "Seasoned Trade lines."

First of all, buying a trade line to qualify for financing, like a home mortgage, is a fraud. You could go to jail or receive a hefty fine.

Second, FICO knows about Seasoned Trade lines and has made adjustments. When those adjustments hit the scoring model lenders use, then those trade lines will become worthless.

Third, you don't need to buy trade lines anyway. Simply ask a family member or someone you've shared an address with, to add you as an AU.

Tell them you don't need or want a card, but you want your credit score to benefit from their good credit history.

Advantages

Typically, unless you get added as an authorized user from a family member or a friend, people will want to charge you like the strategy of piggybacking on other people's positive credit accounts has become well known. It's pretty standard for people to pay to be added to positive aged trade lines, companies exist and thrive on brokering these positive accounts to clients who need a boost in credit for funding purposes. This practice is 100% legal. The primary account holder can add authorized users by simply calling their credit card companies.

(Note to non-US readers: While this works in the US, it does not work in all countries. For example, this strategy does not work in Canada.)

Disadvantages

Being added as an authorized user for someone else's card isn't always good. Their history of credit payment on that card will influence your credit score. If the primary user has defaulted on a couple of payments, it will lower your credit score. On the other hand, if the primary user makes prompt payments and maintains a low balance on the card, it will improve your credit score. The primary user's credit behavior will directly influence your credit score.

This is a strategy that could backfire if the original holder of the account does not make the monthly payments on time. If the original account holder does not pay monthly payments, the late fees not only appear on their report, but they also appear on yours, as well. It might also be advisable to find out if the person you intend on partnering up with has a low percentage of credit utilization.

The simple fact is that you should know that while becoming an authorized user could help you build your credit score; it does come with its risks should the strategy fall flat or go in a way that you did not intend. This is why you should be sure that the original account holder is someone who has a great track record of paying their credit bills on time.

If you're an authorized user on the account, it gets reported on your credit no matter what. Many people have their credit ruined by a spouse or parent going into bankruptcy or not paying their credit card bills. If your name is on any credit cards that belong to people that may not pay their bills, ask them to take your name off immediately!

Chapter 8. What the Lawyers Don't Want You to Know

Listed herein are what credit repair companies don't want you to know and some myths about Credit.

1. It Will Remain on Your Credit Report for Years

A bankruptcy filing will remain a permanent stain on your credit report for seven to ten years, which may have a devastating effect on your potential credit-obtaining ability.

2. Bankruptcy Filing Becomes Public Domain

Bankruptcy is a legal process that ensures it becomes a public record when you file for bankruptcy.

That means that your name and other personal information will appear in court records accessible to the public (including companies, banks, clients, or even potential employers).

3. Filing Doesn't Erase All Debt

Bankruptcy courts have the power to eliminate certain unsecured debts, such as medical bills and credit card balances, but student debt still has to be repaid in full (unless you enroll in any of the loan forgiveness services of the federal government).

4. Filing Is Expensive for Those Without Money

You are filing for bankruptcy because you don't have enough money to pay for payments and debt mounting.

Rates vary by location, but it can take as long as three or five years to conclude a bankruptcy filing, with attorney fees ranging between $2,200 to $3,200 anywhere.

5. Good Luck Finding A Decent Home Loan Any Time Soon

The reality that bankruptcy filers face far harder hurdles in securing a mortgage loan hardly comes as a surprise in a banking world where banks are already skittish about loaning money for a home.

It can take a new bankruptcy filer up to four years before they are accepted for another mortgage loan, according to the Home Buying Institute. Even the Federal Housing Administration needs borrowers to wait at least two years before they can qualify for an FHA home loan after they declare bankruptcy.

There are so many different pieces of information floating around about credit, a lot of which are just myths. We live in an age of information but one of the drawbacks of this is that with so much information, it can be hard to weed out the facts from the myths. Adhering to some of these myths can hurt your credit health.

The first myth that I want to talk about is that having good credit means you have unnecessary debt. I cannot stress enough how untrue this is, it just comes down to understanding how it all works and using it to your advantage, and most importantly, using it responsibly. As referenced early on, having no credit is just as bad as having poor credit, and many people fall into this category because they are always taught from a young age that "credit and credit cards are evil" or "people only use credit when they cannot afford something." This line of thinking is outdated and detrimental when you reach a point where you need to utilize credit. Credit is a great tool, but it requires self-control. Credit cards should be treated as debit cards; only pay for what you can afford, and things you were going to buy anyway such as gas and groceries, and then pay them in full every month to build your credit. If you already spend $60 on gas on your debit card every month, putting that same amount on your credit card and then paying it off does not result in you losing any money or going into debt, it only helps you increase your credit score. However, if you get a credit card and start buying things you cannot afford like expensive clothes and jewelry, the blame falls on you for lacking self-control, not on the company that gave you the credit card.

Another common myth, and reason that many people avoid credit cards in particular, is that you have to pay an excessive amount of money in interest. This is a myth because while credit cards do have an interest, it only applies when you carry a balance on your credit card for longer than one month. As I mentioned before, the goal is only to charge what you can afford, and therefore you can pay your card in full every month. By doing this you will only have the positive effect of building your credit and you will never have to pay any interest.

The third myth is that carrying a small balance on your credit card will help your score. This is completely untrue, as this will result in interest payments due to that revolving balance. There is a myth that lenders may close an account if it has not been used for an extended time. However, using the card often and paying it off will prevent this from happening. It will also prevent you from paying any interest at all which makes it the best method to utilize.

One of the factors of your credit score is each hard inquiry and how they will lower your score. This has sparked the myth that every time you check your credit score, your score will suffer. This is true for hard inquiries, but there is also what is known as a soft inquiry. A soft inquiry is typically when you check your credit information via an online service or through your bank for free. You can check your credit information fifty times per day, and you will see no impact on your score because a soft inquiry does not hurt you. Therefore, it is important to keep an eye on your credit regularly as it will not have any consequences. If there are any mistakes on your report that are negatively affecting you, you can catch them quickly and file a dispute to get them removed.

Another popular myth I want to cover is that having too many credit cards is a bad thing. It goes back to self-control and understanding that you should not be spending money you do not have just because you have the credit available to you.

We talked about how credit utilization is a high impact factor in your credit score, so having several credit cards will increase your total available credit line which will, in turn, boost your credit score. Simply having a larger amount of credit available to you will help you because it shows lenders that you can manage a large amount of money without spending it on things you do not need and cannot afford.

The final myth that you may have heard is that you need a perfect credit score of 850 to get the lowest interest rates when buying a home or car. A score of 850 or anything over 800 is honestly really just good for bragging rights. Generally, a score of 720 and above is what you want to strive for. When you apply for a car loan or a home loan, the interest rate can only be as low as the lender can allow. If the best interest rate they can offer you is around 3%, the person who has a score of 740 will typically get the same benefits as the person who has an 850 score. It is not important to strive for a perfect score, just follow the habits outlined in this book and your score will inevitably rise to high levels.

Chapter 9. How Credit Cards Effect Your Score

Credit cards are a great way to build up your score and get access to all sorts of perks. But credit cards can also be a double-edged sword, especially if you're not paying off the balance every month. If you ever miss out on a payment deadline or accumulate too much debt, your interest rate and credit score will start plummeting like an airplane.

It is about how credit cards affect your credit scores. I break down all the factors that will affect your credit score and explain how to fix them.

Credit Card Payment History

Your payment history is one of the most important factors that determine your score. Your available credit is a part of this, too. A lower amount of available credit on your credit card will hurt you, because it shows that you're using too much of your available credit. If you have a low amount of available credit and a high balance on it, like more than 50% or so, it also looks bad to creditors and your score will drop. On the other hand, if you pay your balances in full every month and keep your overall usage percentage low, then this will be a good thing for your score.

A common mistake people make is paying their credit card balances too low every month. In this case, your available credit will be too low if the amount you use is very low and your balance is high. For example, if you have a $1,000 balance on your card and you pay only $200 a month on it, this will give the appearance to creditors that you are using far less of your available credit compared to someone who has a $10,000 balance on their card and pays twice (or three times) that much in each payment. Be careful to make sure your available credit is not too low.

Credit Card Length of History

The length of your credit history is also very important. The longer the better. All new credit cards you get are going to be added to the total number of all the accounts you've had in the past, and this number will determine your length of history. As long as you only have good credit, this will show that you're a responsible borrower and it will help you get a better score.

Credit Card Credit Limit Amounts

The size or amount of each card's limits also determines the overall total amount of debt on all your accounts, which is part of your score calculation. If you carry a balance on your card that you can't pay off, this is not good for your score. However, if you have enough credit on the card to cover all the balances and do not have any leftover funds, then this will help build up your score as well. Credit limits are determined by each individual lender and can vary greatly from person to person.

Late Payment Fees

Credit reporting agencies like TransUnion and Experian penalize people with high-interest rates for paying late. In fact, they will separate out people who pay late on one charge from those who have a history of paying late everywhere to determine how likely it is that these people will be unable to keep up with their payments in the future. The higher the interest rate, the more likely you will be separated out in the future.

FICO scores are designed to help credit bureaus separate out these late-paying customers by charging them an additional fee. This is not real credit scoring, and it can negatively affect your score if you continue to pay late and do not show that you have started paying on time again.

Maxed-Out Credit Cards

Your available credit limits can also be limited by your maxed-out limits – all the credit limits that you've reached on all your cards combined. When you reach this limit, you may reach a point where paying one card off will cause your available limit to get temporarily reduced or even cut off completely.

The best way to combat this is to apply for a new card and take out a smaller limit. You'll then be able to pay off the old one and have an extra $500 in available credit on it. If you've maxed out the higher limit, you may want to go back down a notch to something lower so that you can remove that card from your credit history and potentially avoid that fee altogether.

Credit Life Experiences (Q Scores)

If you've had several short-term or missed payments, your FICO scores will continue penalizing you for negative information about your track record. This is because they use a proprietary credit scoring system called FICO Q Scores to look at your overall payment history in order to predict how you will behave in the future. The longer it takes you between payments, the more you will be penalized by creditors and credit bureaus.

This is due to another type of scoring system called FICO Q Scores that determines how risky it is for a creditor to loan money to you based on whether or not they think you'll pay them back. PRBC (payment rates, reporting balances, charge-offs) scores are the main components that determine your FICO Q Score, which includes factors such as late-payment fees.

If you have a low FICO Q Score, it means that creditors consider you to be a risk, and they are less likely to try giving you more credit if they deem you to be too risky. This is how your score can actually increase after paying off your balances because it will show creditors that you can be responsible for your payments.

FICO Scores vs. Vantage Scores

Vantage Scores are another type of credit scoring system that was designed by the three major credit bureaus (Equifax, Experian, and TransUnion) as a way to compete with FICO scores from a competitor named Fair Isaac Corp. However, there are some notable differences between the two score types.

The biggest difference is that Vantage Scores are designed to be used by the credit bureaus, not creditors. Therefore, they do not have any real impact on whether or not you get approved for credit cards or other lines of credit. Instead, they are only used to help creditors determine how risky it is for them to lend money to you based on your overall history. A high score in this case does not automatically mean that you'll get a high FICO score.

Differences between FICO Scores and Vantage Scores: Credit Bureaus designed them: Vantage Scores were designed by the three major credit bureaus. They can be used by creditors, but aren't required.

FICO scores are designed by Fair Isaac Corp., which is a third-party credit reporting agency. They are used by creditors.

FICO scores are also used by the credit bureaus as a measure of how risky it will be for them to lend you money, but this has no impact on whether or not you get approved for credit. Credit scoring model: Vantage Scores use a scoring model that is based on 300 to 850 points whereas FICO scores use 300 to 850 points.

Under the new scoring model, Vantage Scores consider your payment history more heavily than credit limits.

Under the old model, FICO scores considered credit limits more heavily than payment history. They are used in conjunction with each other: You need a score that is at least as high as your FICO score to be approved for a credit card.

FICO scores continue to be used by creditors to determine if you are going to get approved for a line of credit, and also if you will get charged interest on it. They use these scores as a way to compare you to other applicants or customers. You are not required to have a FICO score: Your credit history is not scored in the Vantage Score credit scores.

Your payment history is not scored in the Vantage Score credit scores. Vantage Scores are sometimes used by other creditors. FICO scores can be viewed by anyone: The credit bureaus also provide information on your FICO score to anyone who requests it, as well as to your creditors or prospective employers who ask for it. You don't have to pay for having your FICO score checked: You don't get charged anything by the credit bureaus for checking your FICO score, and you also don't have to pay anything if you order a copy of your Vantage Score report.

Free No cost or obligation to order. FICO scores are free, but the credit bureaus charge a fee for providing your Vantage Score. Your report is randomly generated by the credit bureaus and won't contain any identifying information about you, like your name, address, or Social Security number. Unfortunately, some people have reported that the Vantage Score they receive is not a complete and accurate copy of their actual score. Also, note that you don't have to pay anything to check your FICO score.

How Your FICO Score Is Used by Creditors

A creditor may choose to use a different credit scoring system than the one you were given, so they can compare you to others who have applied to be creditors or had existing debts and lines of credit. Creditors are not required to use the same scoring system as the one that is used by third-party credit reporting agencies like TransUnion and Experian. They use their own scoring systems in order to set up their own approval criteria, which won't be designed using the same methodologies or risk assessments as a Vantage Score.

FICO scores are only required to be used in order to meet the requirements of a creditor's own credit policies and practices, such as:

The creditor's minimum credit score requirement for applicants who apply for loans from them; The number of approvals or denials that the creditor gives out; The amount and type of interest that will accrue on a particular line of credit or loan; The amount they will charge you in late fees and penalties if you don't pay off your debts on time; and Any other factors that the lender has decided to add.

For instance, if you want to apply for a credit card with your bank and they decide to use their internal scoring system instead of FICO scores, you might have to pay a $500 deposit to use their card. In addition, there is no guarantee that the card issuer will let you build up your own history with them by making payments on time and paying off your balances without incurring heavy debts.

In this case, they could be using a proprietary credit scoring system that helps them determine if they will grant you access to any lines of credit or not. This scoring system is referred to as an internal scoring model. If they choose to apply your credit history and payment history to their own scoring model, then they will use information from the three major credit reporting agencies, such as TransUnion and Experian.

A large number of creditors are using this method right now. Alternatives like FICO scores are only required by some loan companies and credit card issuers for some types of consumers. This will change over time as more lenders come up with their own scoring systems or switch to another system altogether for consumer approval decisions.

Chapter 10. Debt-Snowball Method

The snowball strategy for credit recovery is a concept that involves first paying off small debts before the large debts to be covered are all that is left. This follows the same idea as creating a snowball, where you have a small ball that eventually develops into a bigger one to start with. In principle, the snowball strategy is perfect because it allows you a chance to see your debts go away one by one. However, this mechanism is not necessarily optimal. Here's a look at how the snowball strategy works so that you can decide if you might want to try something.

The Purpose of the Snowball Method

The snowball strategy is intended to motivate you to continue paying off your debts by encouraging you to see them get paid off. You can at least cross the bill off your list every month if you start with a small credit card. That will make you feel accomplished, and it will give you the confidence you need to continue to pay off your bills. You can pay off another debt over the next few months and then another debt before all you have left one big debt to pay off each month. This will alleviate a lot of your tension, and it should allow you to concentrate more effectively on fixing your loan.

The Downside of the Snowball Method

In principle, the snowball approach is perfect, but it does have a drawback. Large loans demand interest on more money, and that can lead you to pay a lot more over time. You could be shelling out hundreds of additional dollars that you might have avoided by paying big loans first if you leave those loans until the end. You might try to do a reverse snowball strategy, but that might not give you results fast enough to make you feel confident about repairing your reputation. That is why you have to spend more money on this method because it is relatively insignificant in many cases.

How to Use the Snowball Method Effectively

You need to determine the amount of interest you have to pay on various loans if you want to use the snowball approach to your advantage. You must first remember to pay off the 20 percent card if you have five credit cards with a 6 percent interest rate and then one with a 20 percent interest rate. The equilibrium doesn't begin to spiral out of control in that way. Try dividing the payments between the high-interest card and the small balance one if you still want to start with the smallest balance you have. That way, without making the bills piling up at the other end, you can always get everything paid off.

You may also look for some of the high-interest loans to be converted to a low-interest credit card to pay off. You will be able to use the snowball method to its full potential if you do not have to worry about the interest rate. This is rarely the case, but it is something you might benefit from if it works for you. Check out your credit card options to see if there is some way to reduce the interest you pay right now.

Difference between Debt Snowball and Debt Avalanche

By using the debt avalanche strategy, another way to pay off the debt is. This method reverses the order in which you pay off the debt by focusing on the loans or credit cards with the highest interest rates rather than the ones with the lowest balances.

The theory is that you'll save more money on interest by removing loans with the highest interest rates first. However, the actual difference might not be a lot.

If maximizing your savings is your top priority, use the debt avalanche process. But if you like the idea of getting rid of balances more easily by first concentrating on the small ones, use the debt snowball technique.

When Should You Use the Debt Snowball Method?

There is no one-size-fits-all approach to your debt payments. Where one strategy for a friend or family member might work, another may be a better match for you. Here are some situations where the best technique to use could be the debt snowball method:

- Any credit cards you want to close. The debt snowball strategy will help you pay them off quickly if you want to decrease your exposure to credit card debt and those balances are smaller than other loans. You can close the account after that and prevent yourself from once again racking up a balance.

You're trying to reduce the ratio of debt to profits. When applying for new credit, your debt-to-income ratio (DTI) is an important factor, especially with mortgage loans. You'll fully delete them from the DTI equation by removing loans with lower balances, making it easier to get approved for an auto loan or mortgage if you need it.

- You have a hard time remaining inspired. It can be a monumental challenge to pay off debt, and it can be impossible to keep on track if you go without getting rid of any balances for years. You'll begin to see improvement faster in the process by removing your lowest balances first, which will motivate you to stick to your strategy.

During the process, keep an eye on your credit.

Check your credit scores frequently as you focus on paying down your debt to keep track of your success and just to make sure you don't hit any snags. It may stop your progress if you pay off a debt to boost your reputation, and inaccurate or false information is applied to your credit reports. And if you don't catch such stuff early, over time, it might do more harm.

It won't happen overnight to eradicate debt and boost your credit history. But you could save years of time and interest payments if you're patient and stick to your plan, all of which you can invest in working towards practical and exciting financial targets.

Conclusion

For everyone, the snowball strategy is not right, but it might be right for you. If you feel exhilarating after paying off the first debt, give it a try and see. In no time, you will be curious enough to try it again.

Chapter 11.   How to Overcome Credit Card Debt?

What is a Credit Card Debt?

When you incur a credit card debt, you actually keep borrowing money every month, and that is why it is also known as revolving debt. But it is only good until you have the capacity to repay them but when you can't, the debt keeps accumulating. When compared to the loan accounts, you can actually keep using your credit card accounts for an indefinite period of time. In simpler terms, there is nothing that the company can seize, like a house or a card, even when you have failed to repay them. But yes, if you are not able to repay the money you borrowed from the credit card, it is going to affect your credit score drastically.

How Is Credit Card Debt Accumulated?

When you get a credit card, you will see that there will be a due date within which you have to clear the entire balance that you have accumulated on your credit card, and if you fail to do so, you will be accumulating debt. There is a term called APR or Annual Percentage Rate and this is a rate of interest that is charged on your debt when it keeps accumulating one month after the other. The APR that you will be charged may not be the same as someone else's and this is because it keeps differing with your credit history, the bank issuer, and also the type of card that you have.

The benchmark fed funds rate of the Federal Reserve and the prime rate of the credit card interests is somewhat tied, and that is the average value. The credit card debt will increase or decrease with respect to any changes in the target rate made by the Fed.

Now, I want to give you an even clearer picture of how this debt accumulates. For starters, there is a minimum payment that you will have to pay every month whenever you use your credit card to make purchases. This payment is calculated based on a certain percentage (with some additional interest charges) of your balance. If you pay this amount in full, then well and good, but if you don't, then you will be liable to interest. So, the interest will increase if you pay even lesser. The reason behind this is that the nature of credit card interests is compounding so the interest keeps accruing. Thus, if you take a longer time to clear off the debts, then you will owe a huge amount of money to the company, which is much more than what you actually owed before.

What Happens After 7 Years?

This is basically a time limit until which a record is shown in a credit report. But there are certain other negative issues that will stay in your credit report even after seven years, for example, certain judgments, tax liens that are unpaid, and bankruptcy.

But you also have to keep in mind that if any debt is unpaid, then it is not exactly going to vanish even after seven years. Even if the credit report does not list it, you will still owe that money to the lender.

There are several other legal ways that can be implemented by lenders, creditors, and debt collectors to collect the debt that you haven't paid. Some of these methods include a court giving permission to garnish your wages, sending letters, calling you, and so on. One thing that you benefit from because of this seven- years rule is that when the debt is no longer visible on your credit report, it cannot affect your credit score. Thus, you can actually have a better chance of gaining back a good score. Another thing to keep in mind is that this seven-year term is only for the negative information on your report and not the position information because they will stay on the report forever. You should keep an eye out after the seven-year mark as to whether the credit bureaus have removed that information or not. They usually do it automatically, but in case they don't then you will have to raise a dispute.

Many people have this question of what happens to their debt if they accidentally die. Well, in that case, it will be your estate that will be used to pay the debt off. Remember that the debt will not be shoved in someone else's hand in your family because whatever money you owe, it is your debt and not anyone else's. And so, whatever you had, like your accounts and assets will then be used for clearing the debt. And after that, if anything remains from your assets, your heir will receive it.

How to Eliminate Credit Card Debt?

Start Eliminating High-Interest Debts First

When you are trying to eliminate your credit card debt, the biggest obstacle that will stand in your way are the ones that carry a very high rate of interest. Sometimes, the rate of interest can even be in double- digits, sometimes as high as 22%. In that case, paying it off can be a really difficult task. But the reason why I am asking you to start eliminating them first because when you will have cleared these debts, you will have a greater amount of money left in your hand at the end of each month.

Another thing that you could do, but only if you have enough credit available, is to apply for a new credit card. But this should be a zero-interest one. Once you get it, transfer the balance to eliminate the high-interest debt. Yes, I know that some of you might be thinking that it is not a sensible thing to do to apply for another credit card and that is why I will be asking you to get it only if you think you have enough self-restraint not to go buy a bunch of stuff that you don't need.

Keep Making Small Payments

Quite contrary to the technique I mentioned above is another technique which is called the snowflake technique. With this process, you will be making small payments towards your debt every time you get some extra cash in hand. Whatever payment you are making, it does not matter as long as you keep paying.

You can pay $10, or you can pay $20 but at the end of the year, you will find that you have reduced about $1000 simply by paying such small amounts almost every day, even if you are paying $2 on any particular day.

People often ignore this method, thinking that it will be only small amounts but you should not make the mistake of overlooking these small amounts as they have quite the power in them. When you are making these small payments, it would feel as if they are not even leaving any dent but with time, they will sum up and cause a considerable effect on your debt.

Preventive Measures to Avoid Credit Card Debt

Have an Emergency Fund

Think about a situation when you have encountered a problem that requires you to spend a lot of money, for example, a car repair or job loss, or medical emergencies. In such a situation, what you need is an emergency fund, but when people don't have that, they resort to credit cards for help.

But why arrive at such a situation when you can build an emergency fund that will cover at least six months' expenses. A fund of this size will help you to figure out any small expenses that crop up overnight. Take your time to build your emergency fund so that you do not have to rely on debt ever.

But Only Those Things That You Can Afford

When you have a credit card in hand, it can get really tempting, and you start buying whatever you think you want. If not, then don't buy it now. Make a goal to save the money required for purchasing that item instead of buying it on credit.

Don't Transfer Balance If Not Necessary

Some people have this habit of clearing their balance with a higher credit card but such repeated balance transferring can actually backfire on you. When you keep transferring balanced without keeping track of your activities, you might end up with an ever-increasing balance and you will also have to clear the fee requires for all those transfers.

Try Not Taking out a Cash Advance

Sometimes, you may be in the moment, and you were not thinking clearly so, you decide to take a cash advance. Moreover, you will have to realize that you are getting into credit card debt if you have started earning cash upfront. The moment you see it happening, you will have to start working on that emergency fund and also tweak your budget.

Lastly, I would like to say that no matter how many measures you take, try avoiding increasing your credit cards unnecessarily because the more the number of credit cards, the more you will have to stop yourself from overspending.

Chapter 12.   How to Fix Your Credit Yourself in 9 Easy Steps?

Repairing your credit takes nine steps, each of which will be deliberated in greater detail in the next few pages.

1. Obtain a copy of your credit report from the three major credit bureaus (Experian, Trans Union Corp., and Equifax).
2. Highlight all negative items.
3. Challenge each of the negative items.
4. Request an updated credit report; check to ensure that some of the negative items were removed.
5. Repeat steps 2-4 once every two months until no additional items are removed.
6. Prepare a consumer statement disputing each of the remaining negative items, and request that the Credit Bureau include the statement in your credit file.
7. Request that each Credit Bureau furnish you with the names and addresses of each creditor still reporting a negative entry for your account.
8. Contact each of these creditors and attempt to negotiate a settlement.
9. Request that updated copies of your credit report be sent to anybody who received your credit report in the past six months.

These steps are all based on the rights granted to consumers through the Fair Credit Reporting Act (FRCA). As you implement the steps outlined above do note that the FCRA will not protect any request, challenge, or consumer statement that can be proven to be frivolous in nature.

It is highly unlikely that this charge will be made by a creditor or credit bureau, as they know that your defense can be that you were simply acting according to your understanding of your rights as granted by the FCRA.

Step One: Get a Copy of Your Credit Report

Before you can start to fix your credit report, you must first figure out what it contains. If you still have the credit reports that I suggested you get at the beginning of this book, go to step 2. If you don't have a copy of your report, then do the following:

Contact the three major credit bureaus, Experian Inc., Trans Union Corp., and Equifax Inc., to see which agency has a file on you. You might also want to contact other local credit bureaus, because there may be several different versions of your credit report floating around. It is a good idea to start with the three major credit bureaus and deal with others later.

Although you may save $8.00, in your effort to repair your credit, you don't need any unnecessary credit denials added to your credit report at this time. This is the exact kind of information that you are trying to erase from your file. However, if you don't have the $24.00 necessary to buy all three copies of your credit reports, this is an option.

There are other ways of learning about your credit report. Instead of the letter request, you can call the Credit Bureau and make an appointment to assess your credit file in person. It is advisable that you wait for the Credit Bureau to tell you everything they know about your credit history before you volunteer any potentially damaging information to other parties.

Step Two: Note All Negative Items on the Report

Each Credit Bureau has its own way of organizing its credit reports. Make sure that you read and understand all the information they send on how to read their report. It is up to you to determine which entries are damaging.

Such items may include a different social security number, incorrect name or spelling of your name, wrong addresses, and the excessive number of inquiries, charge-offs, late payments, judgments, or anything else that will keep you from being granted new credit.

Perhaps your record was confused with another customer who has a similar name or social security number. Maybe the negative information is outdated, beyond the seven-year legal reporting limit imposed by the FCRA.

Step Three: Challenge Each of the Negative Items

Send letters to each Credit Bureau, challenging each of the negative items on your report, even though they may be true. The Fair Credit Reporting Act (FRCA) states that any credit item that is challenged by a consumer must be proven by the creditor in order to be considered verified.

If this re-verification is not completed in a timely manner (approximately 30 days) or if the challenge goes unanswered, the affected negative credit items must be completely deleted from your file, never to reappear.

Note: Do not challenge more than four items at a time. Challenging more than four may cause the Credit Bureau to deem your challenge frivolous and deny your challenge.

Your challenges can be based on the argument that:

- You never made late payments to that account
- The account is not yours
- You don't remember the facts as stated on your credit report
- You don't remember applying for the credit card

There may be other arguments applicable to your particular situation. The challenging process works very well because there are many factors working to your benefit:

- Certain negative items cannot be proven because they were legitimately in error and should have never been reported in the first place
- Credit denials are often thrown out by creditors soon after they are received. As such, these items are generally not reconfirmed. Also, if the item is over two years old, there is a good chance that these records are not retained by the creditor.

If you have already paid off the account, the creditor will probably not want to be bothered and will not respond to the challenge.

A creditor might not respond within the time constraints set by the credit bureau in accordance with the FCRA's guidelines, generally about 30 days.

There is also the element of human error that can come into play (i.e., they may lose the challenge report, can't find the proof, things get lost in the mail, etc.) and result in a non-response by the creditor. The end result: the items are removed from your report. So, the odds are in your favor.

Step Four: Receive an Updated Credit Report

Within one month of challenging any negative items, you should receive an updated copy of your credit report (hopefully without some of the old negative items). If you have not received your new report within 6 weeks, call the credit bureau and remind them that you are waiting for the new copy of your credit report.

Step Five: Repeat this Procedure Once Every Two Months

Keep repeating steps 2 through 4 every two months until no additional items are removed as a result of your challenges. If the remaining creditors are determined to reconfirm their claims and continue to do so over and over again, it is time to move on to the next step.

Step Six: Prepare a Consumer Statement

Prepare a 100-word statement of dispute for each of the remaining negative items, and have the Credit Bureau include these statements in your credit file. These statements will show that the situation is still in dispute and that there is another side to the story. You won't be declared unworthy of credit based on these claims, because they are still pending.

Step Seven: Request the Names and Addresses of Each Creditor

Explain to the Credit Bureau that there are still many mistakes on your credit report and that you would like to contact the creditors in question directly. Request that the Bureau send you the names, addresses, and phone numbers of each creditor still reporting a negative entry for your account.

Step Eight: Contact Each Creditor and Negotiate a Settlement

Negotiations between each creditor may differ depending on the circumstances. Creditors of unsecured loans are motivated to settle because after a certain amount of time these accounts are written off as a total loss; any payments would be considered to be "found" money, so you will probably have a very willing negotiating partner.

Step Nine: Ask That They Send Out Your Updated Credit Report

When your credit report is as clean as it's going to get, contact each Credit Bureau one more time. Request that updated copies of your credit report, be sent to all the creditors who received a copy of your credit report within the past six months.

Chapter 13. How to Maintain It and Mindset

Many folks suffer a financial crisis at some point. They may have to deal with overspending, loss of a job, a family member, or personal illness. These financial problems can be and usually are, overwhelming. To make these situations worse, most people don't even know where to begin to solve these financial dilemmas. Our goal here is to shine some light on the strategies to help get youth Accumulating basic consumer debt will chain you into slavery and you could possibly spend your life held down by your own obligations to repay these loans. Who do you work for? I don't care what you say; the real answer is your creditors if you are currently stuck paying the debt. There are many forms of "dumb debt" you can get trapped into. We are all sold images and lifestyles hundreds of times per day to provoke this materialistic behavior.

The person or institution lending you the money is trusting that you have the ability to hold up your end of the bargain, basically. Sometimes, it may seem impossible to live your life without the option to get a credit, but this is what bad credit eventually leads to. Since your ability to repay a loan has been affected, either by the inability to pay or a series of misunderstandings, other lenders will become skeptical when it comes to granting you a new credit.

But how do you get a credit in the first place? What is the process you have to go through to loan money? Well, it all starts with a credit application to a bank or some other party that has the necessary finances. Your application is reviewed and, if they think there won't be a problem with getting their money back, you sign a contract and get your money in no time. This application contains a large amount of relevant information about yourself such as your employment situation, your monthly income, and other credits or obligations like rent, for instance. The application you submit to a lender is used to obtain a credit report from one or several reporting agencies, depending on how much money you need. These two documents are given scores and, if your score is enough, you'll get the money you need. If not, your application will be rejected. If you don't fall into any of these categories, then a judgment call has to be made by the person or institution providing the credit. The more "good credit" criteria you meet, the more likely it is that you will get your credit.

However, there are several things that you must consider before you put yourself into the category of citizens unaffected by bad credit. First of all, the lenders look for certain things in your application, such as an up-to-date credit report and no late payments on your other financial obligations. They are interested to see if you've had a job for more than a year and have a stable income, as well as a stable residence. They also evaluate the situation of your utility and phone bills and appreciate it if you include information about additional credit cards or other types of cards. It is not only banks and money lenders that look at this type of information. Sometimes, if you want to get a new job, your employer will conduct this type of research too, so maintaining a good credit is crucial in these troubled times we live in.

What type of credit should you get? That depends on what you plan to do with the money. The most used types of credit are secured and signature credits. For smaller loans, there's no need for that, as no institution would like to end up with a store of household items, so they lend you money or issue a credit card in your name simply based on the strength of your credit so far.

There is hope; you as the borrower have many options to get rid of debt. You can take advantage of budgeting and other techniques, such as debt consolidation, debt settlement, credit counseling, and bankruptcy procedures. You just have to choose the best strategy that will work for you. When choosing from the various options, you have to consider your debt level, your discipline, and plans for the future.

The Good Debt

Some people find it hard to live debt-free at least they will have some debt to pay off. While some debts are discouraged, good debt is considered as the money you borrow so that you can pay for things that you really need or things that increase in value. On the flip side, bad debt is one that arises from things that you only want and often decreases in value.

Of course, debt isn't a bad thing; it's just how you use the money that matters.

For a good debt, you will always have a good reason to justify it, and a developed plan for paying it so that you can clear the debt as quickly as possible.

An individual with good debt will also have the cheapest methods of borrowing money. They will do this by looking at the borrowing method, rate of interest, credit amount, and charges that are appropriate to them.

Sometimes, it may imply a deal with the least possible interest rate, but sometimes, it may not.

Examples of good debt

Paying for medical care. There is no fixed amount of money to borrow to ensure your loved one stays healthy. You can manage to pay off the money you borrow, but it is impossible to replace a human life. If a person requires expensive treatments to ensure they remain healthy, this would be an acceptable debt, no matter what.

Borrow money for education. When you apply for a student loan debt, you aren't making the wrong decision. In general, people with college degrees earn more income in their life than those without a degree.

And applying for a student loan so that you can support the education of your child defeats the idea of using your savings. After all, you cannot borrow money to pay for your savings. Multiple government programs provide low-interest student loans, and you can always cut student loan interest on your taxes.

Taking out a mortgage on a home. Taking a loan of this amount can be overwhelming, but purchasing a house creates ownership in something that will house you, and generate some retirement money. Even while you struggle to clear your debt, you may consider it an advantage to put any available liquid cash as a deposit, though it may not be the right choice.

A home mortgage interest is cut on your taxes, and the rate of interest is lower on your home loan than on the credit card. In other words, it is important to have money to pay for other expenses instead of credit.

Though purchasing a house was initially considered a strong, future-proof investment, certain homeowners do find themselves on the wrong side on their home mortgage loan. They owe banks more than the value of their homes. However, strategic planning, purchasing only what you can afford, and maintaining low interest by having good credit may allow you to purchase a home that one day you will own completely.

Buying a car. If you don't have public transport in your area, or you cannot manage to get someone with whom you can carpool, then you may have to consider buying a car. An auto loan can either be "good" or "bad," but the main thing is to ensure that the auto loan is a good debt, so look for the lowest possible rates on your loan. In addition, you need to make a large down payment while ensuring that you remain with some cash on hand just in case you need it.

Your best goal should be to go for a used car model instead of a brand-new one, possibly saving yourself thousands on the sticker price and the interest that is paid throughout the loan.

Business loans. While this may not be seen as good debt, borrowing money to begin a business or expand a business is perhaps a great idea if the business is thriving. After all, you need money to make more money, right?

Sometimes, you may have to borrow capital to employ new people, purchase a new device, pay for advertisement, or even develop the first new widget you designed. The point is that you borrow this money to expand the business or increase income, then this will count as good debt.

What is Bad Debt?

Bad debt is that which depletes your wealth and isn't affordable. Plus, it provides no means to pay for itself.

Bad debts may have no realistic repayment plans and usually deplete when people buy things on impulse. If you aren't sure whether you can repay the money, then don't borrow the money because that will be a bad debt.

Examples of bad debt

The credit card debt. A typical household in the United States has a balance of more than $10,000 on their credit card every month. However, the debt usually increases faster than we may realize and is always used to purchase things that we want instead of need. It is easier to think that you can afford something using a card than paying it with cash.

Borrowing from a 401K. When you ask for money from a 401K program, you will need to chat with the IRS, and if you aren't using the money to purchase a home, you will need to pay the loan in five years. If you fail to pay it back, you risk being charged with a severe penalty. Also, the interest that you pay on the loan will get taxed twice.

You can't get a loan to fund your retirement. For that reason, borrowing money from your retirement plan to use it to pay for anything that isn't part of retirement is a bad idea. You will be putting your retirement at risk when you get a loan from a 401k, so don't make this mistake.

Payday loans. It may appear easy to borrow money from payday loan firms, but it is hard to pay it back. These companies offer loans with very high interest rates. The companies take advantage of the fact that many people need that money. As a result, borrowing a small amount may end up costing you a lot.

Payday loans aren't considered the worst kind of debt that you can take on. If you really need a short-term loan, it is better to go for a cash advance on a credit card rather than borrow money from these firms.

Using consolidation or settlement strategies to pay down debts

Debt consolidation is another strategy that can be used to manage your debts. It involves combining two or more debts at a lower interest rate than you are currently at.

But it is worth doing your research and making some phone calls to see if there is a company that's willing to work with you. If you can lower your monthly bill to a manageable level, at an interest rate that's reasonable, that can make all the difference in handling your debt.

Like many strategies, you have had the option of settling your debts with companies for decades. Lenders always want as much money as you can give them versus being shafted for the entire amount in a bankruptcy. It is just that consolidation and settlement options rose in popularity during the recent financial crisis making it appear in more articles and news pieces than ever before.

If you have savings to pay off your debts, then start with the most expensive. Otherwise, utilize settlement options where you are able to reduce the amount owed if you pay a certain amount right now. As long as the account shows paid in full, with a strong payment history, your scores are going to increase. It doesn't matter if you needed to use debt settlement strategies to make the debt end. It just matters that you have paid the debt off instead of letting it go into arrears.

Chapter 14. How to Remove Extra Names and Addresses from Your Report?

It's not a secret that you have to work hard to get the best credit score possible. It's also not a secret that different businesses use your social security number and address for identity verification. When you are doing your due diligence, you may want to remove these addresses and names from your report if they're showing up on your credit report unnecessarily.

This post will cover what information can be removed from your report, how long it can take, what companies this removes information from, and other considerations like whether or not it affects the accuracy of loans.

Contact Your Credit Reporting Agencies

The first thing you want to do is contact the credit reporting agencies. (Equifax, Experian, and TransUnion) Ask them how to remove information that's on your credit report but that isn't yours. For example: your neighbor's name on file with collections, someone else's collection, or extra addresses. They will likely guide you to their removal process and may show you a form or a link to fill out. You may be able to call them as well if they offer phone support for the removal of such information.

Most of the time the process is simple and just takes a few weeks. You may have to provide documentation of why you want to remove information from your credit report.

If you want the removal to be processed for free, you will need to contact each of the companies and follow their instructions as to how much documentation they require. The minimum amount of documentation required is generally $10 per account/file or $35 for all three. In general, showing a lack of usage of your address and social security number will suffice as evidence that the information shouldn't be on your file in the future.

Note: If you wish to dispute anything that is on your file, such as an item going from good standing (not being charged off) to bad standing (charged off), these are handled separately. So, make sure you contact all three credit reporting agencies and follow their instructions on how to dispute.

How Long Does This Take?

The process can take anywhere from a few weeks to over a year depending on the nature of the information being removed, the number of accounts, and the amount of documentation required. In general, it's not uncommon for removal to be processed within a few months.

A good rule of thumb is that it will take longer if you need to provide extensive documentation like paying off collections balances or demonstrating no usage. It may also take longer if an item is disputed or you're having other issues with your report. There are also certain criteria that need to be met or removed from your report in order to prevent having the issue reappear at a later time.

What Companies Does This Remove Information From?

This will vary depending on what information you're trying to remove from your report. If you want to remove addresses and names, this information is shared among Equifax, Experian, and Transunion. Therefore, it will be removed from all three companies' files. The same applies if you want to remove an old address or name from collections accounts or other bad standing items like charge-offs or late payments. These are available to all three credit reporting agencies and therefore the removal process is likely very similar across all three companies.

If you are trying to remove accounts, collections, or items that don't impact your credit score (for example, old open accounts) you will not be able to remove this information from all three companies. This is because Equifax and TransUnion will not share certain information with Experian. This means that you can only get eliminated from some of the reports at one or two of the companies. If you are trying to get removed from Equifax's report, for example, the removal process will likely be different than if that information was on Experian's report.

If you are looking to have an account, collection, or other information removed from all three companies' credit report, you will need to make sure that is listed only on one of the companies' report.

How Does This Affect the Accuracy of My Loans?

This can be a complicated question since each lender is different and uses varying criteria to determine your score. Some lenders will only pull one of the reports if they are available for a specific address or social security number. Others may not care at all and pull all three if they have access to them. Generally speaking, most lenders use all three credit files and pull from each one equally in order to determine your credit score accurately.

If you are trying to get removed from all three companies, it's possible that your score could be negatively impacted when the removal is processed. This is due to the fact that if profiles are removed, any lender that pulled all three files would not have access to them in the future. Therefore, the information for those specific accounts/profiles won't be available when determining your score. As a result, your score could decrease for a short period of time as other lenders are trying to evaluate your request.

The most common instance that may cause your score to decrease is if you are trying to remove an address that is used by a lender. This is because they may not be able to access the account or profile for the new address if it was previously listed on all three reports. However, since most lenders use all three equally, this shouldn't have a negative impact on your score long term.

What Are the Best Ways to Get Removed from Credit Report Information?

If you want the removal procedure to go as easily as possible, there are a few things you can do to make it go as swiftly as feasible.

1. Identify Which Companies are Requesting the Removal

Make sure that you identify which company you are dealing with so that you know what information they have access to. This is important because it will affect the process of making sure that information is removed from the correct accounts or profiles. As mentioned above, there is a good chance will be able to remove all three reports with one removal request. However, you may need to make specific requests if certain accounts or items only appear on one of the reports.

2. Focus on Removing "Current" Information First

If you have ongoing collections or other items that can be removed, focus on getting those items removed first rather than focusing on past accounts (like old charge-offs). The reason for this is because the new collections or accounts will be listed on the credit report longer than a paid-off account. This means that it will be harder to get removed from the account later on if you previously had it removed but then added it again later.

3. Removing Old Information is Only Necessary If It is Impacting Your Loan Process

The final thing to keep in mind when removing information from your credit file is how this information relates to your loan process. As mentioned above, the removal of old collections and paid accounts won't have any impact on your current loan process if you are making a large purchase today. However, if you are making a home purchase in the near future, it is important that the reports do not show collections or accounts that are more than a few years old.

Having good information on your credit file will help your loan process go smoothly and quickly. However, having old accounts or collections can create negative information for some lenders and may slow down the loan process from you getting to closing on your new home. Therefore, it is important to focus on removing collections and older accounts first. Depending on how particular your lender is about their accuracy, getting a little creative with removing troublesome information can be beneficial to your overall loan process.

Chapter 15.   Delete Inquiries Like the Pros

An inquiry is when a creditor, employer, or insurance company requests to view and examine your credit reports via TransUnion, Equifax, or Experian. You have soft inquiries and hard inquiries, a hard inquiry is when you give consent to any potential creditor to pull your credit reports, and too many hard inquiries will hurt your score. Soft Inquiries are also referred to as a soft pull, this is when you check your own credit, or credit card companies want to look at your score to solicit you for pre-approval offers.

Current creditors often perform soft pulls to issue periodic credit line increases. These acts are both documented by the credit bureaus, no need for you to worry about soft pulls; they will not hurt your credit score no matter how many times you check your own credit. You can opt-out to prevent others from looking at your reports through soft pulls. Hard inquiries will be kept on your credit report for a period of up to 25 months. Allowing too many creditors to pull your credit within a short period of time will damage your chances for new credit as each inquiry can cost you 3-5 points of your fico score, it is best to have no more than 5 inquiries reporting at a time on each credit bureau. Applying for too many accounts will result in you looking too thirsty to obtain credit. The longer an inquiry sits on your credit report, the less it impacts your fico score, but too many recent inquiries will get you automatic denials in the computer underwriting systems of most banks and credit card issuers.

It is never a good idea to request any forms of credit before you plan on financing any big purchase, especially a mortgage. Every point counts when you are looking for low-interest rates on long-term loans. Another way to control inquiries is to understand which credit report will be pulled by certain creditors; you can even direct certain creditors to pull from a bureau of your favor by freezing the others and applying by phone. Perhaps you have the highest score with Equifax, and you know a specific lender that pulls both Equifax and Experian, it would be wise for you to freeze Experian that has the lower fico score, and this allows easy access to your Equifax. Applying for enough credit over the years, I created my own database of which credit bureaus lenders pull from, which can also depend on your city and state. You can also legally freeze and unfreeze any of your credit reports at any time online or over the phone.

How to Delete Inquiries like a Pro

It is very common to see files of clients that have 10, 15, or even 20 inquiries on each credit bureau. Either they have let a car dealership or multiple car dealerships run their credit through multiple banks, or they crossed their fingers and applied for any and every credit line they could think of. Either way, with computers processing most applications, this can be an automatic denial for many credit products, especially for credit cards and loans from prime issuers. Too many recent inquiries only show lenders you are desperate for credit, and banks only lend money to those who appear to not really need it. For those who do have many inquiries, you don't necessarily have to wait 2 years for them to fall off; you can actually question their legitimacy and request that the credit bureaus delete them.

A Permissible Purpose includes the use of the report for the following reasons:

1. With the consumers written authorization.
2. In connection with the extension of credit as a result of an application from a consumer.
3. In connection with the collection of a consumer's account.
4. In making a decision to hire or promote a consumer who has given written permission for the use.
5. In connection with the underwriting of insurance as a result of an application from a consumer.
6. In response to some other legitimate business need arising in connection with a business transaction initiated by the consumer.
7. To determine whether the consumer continues to meet the terms of an account.

With this being said, it is tough for any credit bureau to prove that you actually gave permission for a creditor to view your credit report, especially without a physical application.

Once they forward the dispute to the furnisher, that creditor really doesn't have any interest in going back and forth with you over this disputed inquiry. Once again, they have bigger fish to fry; they have to worry more about those who actually do owe them some money. Most consumers apply online or on the phone these days for accounts, so it is impossible for these furnishers to provide any physical proof that you actually did initiate the inquiry. If you write and send your dispute by mail for multiple inquiries, make sure it is with a demand letter to the credit bureaus first; it can become costly sending certified mail to multiple creditors individually. You can formulate your letter and ask for these 3 simple things:

1. Permissible purpose.
1. Proof that the consumer initiated the inquiry.
2. Written authorization.

Those who pulled your credit cannot provide these three things unless you have an account attached to the inquiry, and if so, I advise that you count your blessings for the approval and don't try to remove it.

Remember, anytime you are disputing inquires you are standing on the grounds that an application in your name was unauthorized, if for any reason you are being ignored or they refuse to delete, you can send a 605B Identity Theft related letter with the support of an automated police report listing all inquiries you are disputing. If you call to dispute, depending on who helps you over the phone, they will want you to report the inquiries as fraudulent, then forward you to the fraud department anyway. After disputing the inquiries, you will have what is called a fraud alert on your credit file as a result. A fraud alert just means that before any credit can be extended to you in the future, they will first have to go through all the necessary steps to assure that you are who you say you are, and not someone attempting to use your identity. If a fraud alert is placed, just remember you will be better off applying for additional credit in person or over the phone until it comes off or you request to delete it by phone that will take up to 48 hours to process. Fraud alerts last 90 days and extended fraud alerts stay on your credit reports for 7 years. Adding your permanent phone number to your fraud alert is the most convenient way to go, I personally suggest that you remove the fraud alert right after you get the inquiries deleted if you plan to submit any applications after. Fraud alerts can help protect your credit otherwise.

With any resistance from the credit bureaus, you can also dispute your inquiries one by one directly with the creditors. They usually won't put up a fight, I prefer to dispute with the credit bureaus first as it is less time demanding than reaching out to every single furnisher responsible for reporting an inquiry if there are many. If for some reason you missed a step or just can't get the results you need, you can threaten or actually sue the furnisher of the inquiry for the violation of section 604 of the FCRA, this violation can reward you with a fine from the defendant. You will never get all the way to court for a matter like this, but as always, have your paper trail.

*Do not repeatedly apply for credit and dispute your inquiries just because you know how, you want to do everything in moderation to not abuse this tactic for yourself.

"Making more money is not always the answer; some people make 7 figures but still live paycheck to paycheck."

Chapter 16. The FUQ'S (Frequently Unasked Questions): Things Everyone Should Know About Their Credit Score.

Frequently Unasked Questions

In life, questions are more important than answers. The reason is that you get a clearer understanding of things when you learn to ask the right questions. So, I called this the Frequently Unasked Questions because this section deals with questions that people want to ask about but is not really what everybody asks, so they assume it is not necessary to know. Just like I have mentioned over and over again in this book, the best way to understand the credit score world is to never assume you know it all. Keep asking and researching, find out information about your credit report, credit score, and how banks make use of your credit history in deciding on your loan requests. Here, I will show you questions you may already know the answers to, but I will take my time to properly explain them and also questions you might have never even thought of yet, but I bet you they will be useful in the long run.

What is the catch in having a good score?

Everyone should be interested in having a good score as this has several advantages. Some of which are, for a case where you would like to take a loan out, it will help you get very favorable conditions. This also supports you in winning the contract for a new apartment. Many property managers do not take the risk and look for solvent tenants in particular who pay the rent on time. These are just a few benefits, amongst many.

What factors influence my credit rating?

When you're shopping, either online or in a fixed shop or supermarket, there's a lot to consider. "Zero percent financing" sounds like a good idea, but bear in mind that this is also a loan. This is not often concluded with the company, where a product is to be bought, but with a cooperating bank. Because "zero-percent financing" is a loan, it is only available to consumers with good credit ratings and has an impact on your score. Paying attention to some hidden costs such as processing fee which is also very important. Either it is online or on the ground, when ordering from mail-order companies, endeavor to pay invoices on time. Otherwise, your score can be affected negatively. A corresponding score means that you can't order on account.

What is the importance of performing scoring procedures?

The scoring procedures are performed most times when you want to borrow. Even if you're using the "zero-percent financing," a scoring is carried out nevertheless. Moreover, scoring plays a major role if a company is to provide a service before you pay for it. This often happens with mobile phone contracts or shipping dealers a lot. However, the score value does not only determines whether a loan is granted to you but on what terms and conditions as well. A customer with a good score will obviously receive better terms and conditions than a customer with a bad one. They can, therefore, be able to ascertain that the customer will repay the credit without hitch or difficulty. This then means that scoring procedures help companies, banks, and as well as service providers, in particular, to assess the risk of a business and be able to hedge it.

How do they compose my personal score?

The scoring process involves, on one part, one's personal data and historical experience on the other. From this, a phantom score is prepared by means of mathematical-statistical methods, allowing indications of the future behavior of the "scanned" person. Including the data and experience values, already included in the evaluation, the socio-demographic data (such as gender, age, the payment experience, known address, etc.), or contract data (such as the number of accounts and credit cards). However, the specific composition of scoring is a whole lot different for each scoring provider and is not made public.

Are credit rating and credit scoring the same?

No, they aren't. Score values deal with the creditworthiness of a group of people. However, the term "creditworthiness" or credit rating is known as the solvency of an individual or a company.

What does score entail?

Scoring helps to predict the behavior of groups of people with similar characteristics. Mathematical-statistical methods are used to calculate scores of a group of people and hence a statement is obtained on the risk of payment default of those people. The assumption most times is that people with the same characteristics will also tend to behave the same manner. Hence, this suggests that scores do not evaluate the creditworthiness of a single person, but rather predict the payment behaviors of a group of people to which a specific person belongs to. In the scoring process, empirical values from the past are applied to make deductions on similar events that play out in the future.

What time was credit scoring born?

Around the late 1950s and early 1960s, banks in the United States of America started working together by sharing their customer data, which included account balances and payment histories especially.

This method was, at first, limited to just small communities.

However, as of the 1970s, several large companies emerged as leaders in credit reporting.

In 1970, the American Congress initially approved the Fair Credit Reporting Act (FCRA) in order to control the manner in which credit verification companies handled personal consumer information. This was the first step towards the regulation of the sector.

In the early 1980s, loans, requests, detailed personal information (including social security numbers, addresses, date of birth), and also payments that are still the basis of the credit valuation were electronically stored.

Why credit scoring? Why does it exist?

The credit history reporting system aids banks in not lending money to customers who have already been over-exposed and tagged as bad payers.

Until less than 80 years ago, the banking sector was a different experience entirely. Then, if you want to borrow money, you had to go into a bank branch and convince a manager one-on-one to grant you a loan. A proof of your income would have been requested from you as well as personal references who could guarantee your reliability. Back then, most loans were taken care of by guarantees, meaning that good collateral had to be offered to pay off the loan.

The commonest example of a loan guaranteed today is the loan for buying a property. In this agreement, the property is still the one that acts as the collateral.

With time, the high availability of credit cards as a comfortable electronic purchasing tool has also cleared the unsecured loan. And even if the unsecured loan were more profitable to banks, it was still very risky because there would be no guarantee for the bank to repay the sum paid if the debtor does not repay the loan.

Because of this, the credit scoring system came into play and was created to enable banks to have a central source of information on prospective customers.

What are the other factors that influence your credit scoring?

Yes, some of which is the average age of your current accounts, recent funding requests, and any collateral that has been pledged against your assets.

Each of these makes up about 10-15% of your credit score.

The longer you have the current account, the better. Also, try to limit the credit requests to no more than two at least every six months. When you have too many credit requests in a short time, it can decrease your credit score as it suggests that you are in desperate need of money.

However, there is an exception for those whose credit requests are of the same nature. This will indicate that you are making an evaluation of a particular expense.

If it happens that these requests occur within a month or so, it will be generally accepted as one request.

What does the personal information in my credit scoring consist of exactly?

Your credit scoring contains all information about you, which includes your name, social security number, address, and information about your financial assets, such as payments histories, balances, and loan applications.

Your credit report majorly contains detailed information on recent activity on your financial accounts. This includes:

- **Credit requests:** whenever you request a credit, either you have been approved or not.
- **Open loans:** the data will have the bank, the loan amount, the loan opening date, the monthly payment amount, and the payment history.
- **Use of credit cards:** data includes the ban, credit limit, account opening date, payment history, and the monthly payment amount.
- **Closed accounts:** a closed account remains on the report for a maximum of up to seven years.
- **Public accounts:** include judicial decisions and bankruptcy declarations.

How do you know you are doing a good job? How do you measure your progress?

As much as your credit report contains all information about your credit history, your credit score remains the best way to measure your progress in building your credit. Your credit score is referred to as the numerical summary of all information contained in your credit report within a particular time. It is the number that lenders and creditors use to decide whether to approve your requests and what interest rate to charge.

There are sites on which you can get your scores free of charge, some of which are creditkarma.com and creditsesame.com. You can also get your for-FICO number for an affordable fee at myFICO.com. This FICO score, especially, is the one most creditor use.

This way, you can regularly monitor your credit score and update yourself on the changes that occur over time in your credit history.

How can I repair my bad credit scoring?

It's the same method for building a good one! Paying bills on time and staying away from debts. The best way to repair your credit is to pay your bills, reduce the level of debt per time and limit demand for fresh loans.

It would take about one or two years of responsible credit management to see your credit score improve exponentially. There are no shortcuts. Stick with this and you will see the change you desire

Chapter 17. How to Protect Your Credit and Credit Monitoring?

Knowing everything you can about the credit card game is important. Almost everyone has a credit card, but few people know how to use it correctly. Chances are you are reading this book because you have already made financial mistakes and you want to fix them. Don't apply for a credit card before you've read the terms. There's more to choosing a credit card than picking a design or a credit card issuer. You need to evaluate the card on other factors as well. Consider what kind of card you want. Do you want a rewards credit card, a regular credit card, a student credit card, or a card that you can transfer a balance to? How you are planning on using a credit card is also something that you need to consider. If you are going to be carrying a balance on the card, look for a low interest rate. Find out what the annual percentage rate (APR) is on the credit card, and also what the grace period is that you can pay your balance in full before you are charged an additional finance charge. Finally, find out what the yearly fees on the card are and what the reward structure is on the card.

Don't Use Credit Cards for Necessities

Do not use your credit cards to pay for things like clothes, gas, and food if you have the cash on hand. Most people find themselves on the road to debt by using their credit in place of cash. If you are using your credit card as a way to build your credit, it can be wise to use it in place of money, as long as you are making sure that you are putting the same amount of money aside from your bank account to put back on your credit card.

If you are using the money on your credit card for groceries and still spending the money that you have in the bank, you are going to find yourself in debt very quickly.

Don't Get into The Habit of Only Making Minimum Payments

By paying only the minimum amount required on an account, you are only putting off the debt that you owe, which also increases the amount of interest you are going to accrue on the account. Usually, minimum payments are only the amount of interest gained on the outstanding balance so you won't even be making payments toward the actual principal debt.

By paying as much as possible toward the balance, you are helping to decrease the amount of the principal debt, which in turn decreases the amount of interest you will pay in the long run.

Don't Use Credit for Things You Can't Pay For

Don't live above your means. If there is an expensive item you want but don't need, it's important to recognize that if you don't have the money for it now, you probably won't have it anytime soon. Wait until you have the money to pay for your purchases before you acquire them.

However, sometimes you need to make a high-ticket purchase because there is an emergency, for example, your fridge dies, or you need a new furnace.

In an emergency, it would be appropriate to use your credit card as long as you are making it a priority to pay the balance on your credit card back down.

Don't Close a Credit Card Account Without Knowing How It Is Going to Impact Your Credit Score

Your credit score may suffer if you close a credit card account. Avoid closing accounts with balances or accounts you've had for many years that have made up a great portion of your credit history.

When you look at your credit report, you are going to be able to see how long you have had a credit account open. It is not a smart idea to close your credit card if you have had it for ten years and it is in excellent standing, especially if all of your other credit cards are newer.

Let Your Creditor Know If You Won't Be Able to Make Your Monthly Payment on Time

Ignoring the situation is not going to make it go away. If you are unable to make a payment on time, contact the company, and discuss available options.

Many times, they will work with you to adjust your due date and waive late fees if you know this will be a one-time problem.

Keep an Eye on Your Utilization

Remember, you want to keep the utilization below 20%. That means that you are going to want to try to keep the amount on your card within 20% of your credit limit. Not only is this going to keep your balance low and more manageable, but it will also help to keep your credit score high. Ask for a Lower Interest Rate If you have maintained or improved your credit and begin to receive offers from other institutions offering you a lower rate than you are currently paying, contact your creditors and ask if they will lower your interest rate.

Review Your Credit Card Statement Thoroughly Every Month Don't assume that everything that is on your credit card statement is accurate. Read through every transaction and ensure that your last payment was applied properly, that you were charged correctly for all your purchases, and that there are no unauthorized charges on your account. Report unauthorized charges to your credit card company immediately and dispute errors within sixty days of them occurring.

Chapter 18.   Reach Your Financial Freedom

Financial freedom is a concept that people love to think about but rarely feel like they can reach.

What Is Meant by Financial Freedom?

Financial freedom has no set definition. However, it typically means that you are living comfortably and saving for retirement and in general. It can also mean that you have an emergency reserve set up. In general, financial freedom can mean whatever you want it to mean for you. For example, a prior college student may not think that financial freedom includes paying off all their student loans. This is because, at least in this day and age, a college student who needs to pay their way realizes they will always be paying off their student loans. However, they might feel that student loans are the only debt they should have. Therefore, being able to pay off credit cards or medical bills leads them to financial freedom.

Some people might feel that financial freedom indicates they have absolutely no debt or loans. This includes them having paid off their mortgage and any car loans. They might also feel that in order to reach financial freedom, they need to be investing in a CD, bond, or even in the stock market.

Other people may feel that financial freedom means they are no longer tied down to a job. They are able to live off of their savings or a passive income, and they are able to retire and enjoy life through traveling.

Credit Cards and Financial Freedom - Is It Safe?

One of the biggest questions people have when it comes to financial freedom is whether they can have any credit card accounts in their name. While you may not owe anything on your credit cards (in fact, you might only owe one which you pay off in full every month), is this still financial freedom? In general, this is completely determined by your definition of financial freedom. However, if you ever find yourself not being able to pay off your credit card every month, this is not financial freedom. In most cases, financial freedom does mean you no longer have any debt, or at least that you are free from unnecessary debt, such as credit cards.

Most people are quick to state that financial freedom and credit cards do not go together simply because they are not safe with each other. This is due to the fact that it is often easy to fall back into thinking you can pay the amount off everything each month and then you become unable to do so. In general, people who reach financial freedom feel that credit cards allow for more of a trap and keep them from ever reaching financial freedom.

However, other people who feel they have reached financial freedom state that as long as you can manage your credit cards wisely, they can be included with your freedom. Some of them also advise that you set up a financial freedom plan. Within this plan, you will state your conditions for using a credit card. Of course, you need to be self-disciplined enough to follow your condition.

The Best Habits to Help You Reach and Protect Your Financial Freedom

When it comes to financial freedom, there are dozens of habits and tips that people provide in order to help you reach your financial freedom. It is important to note that because financial freedom can vary depending on the person's definition, some of the tips and habits might work for you while others may not. You need to find the ones that work best for you, not the ones that other people say are the best. Therefore, I am going to give you a fairly large list as I want you to make sure that you can find some of the best habits and tips so you can not only reach financial freedom but also protect it.

1. Make a Budget

Making and keeping a budget is one of the first steps everyone should take while heading towards financial freedom. Even though you might find yourself changing your budget now and then, as you will add or delete bills or receive a different income, you always want to follow it. Not only will this help you in reaching your financial freedom but continuing to follow your budget will also protect your financial freedom.

Furthermore, creating a monthly budget can make sure that all your bills are being paid and you know exactly where your money is going. For example, you will be able to see how much money you spend on groceries, gas, and eating out at restaurants. This will help you know where you can decrease your spending, which will allow you to save more. There are a lot of great benefits when it comes to creating and sticking with a household budget.

2. Set Up Automatic Savings Account

If you work for an organization that will automatically place a certain percentage of your check into a savings account, take advantage of this. It gives you the idea that you never had the money to begin with, which means you don't plan for it and you won't find yourself taking the money out of savings unless you need it for an emergency. Furthermore, you can set up a separate savings account where this money will go. You can make it, so you rarely see this account, however, you want to make sure that your money is deposited, and everything looks right on your account. But, the point of this account if you do not touch it, even if you have an emergency. Instead, you will set up a different account for an emergency basis.

The other idea to this is you pay yourself first. This is often something that people don't think about because they are more worried about paying off their debt. However, many financial advisors say that you are always number one when it comes to your finances. While you want to pay your bills, you also need to make sure that you and your family are taken care of.

3. Keep Your Credit in Mind Without Obsessing Over It

Your credit score is important, but it is not the most important thing in the world. People often fall into the trap of becoming obsessed over their credit score, especially when they are trying to improve it. One factor to remember is that your credit score is typically only updated every so often. Therefore, you can decide to set time aside every quarter to check on your credit report. When you do this, you not only want to check your score, but you also want to check what the credit bureaus are reporting. Just like you want to make sure everything is correct on your bank account; you want to do the same thing for your credit report.

4. It Is Fine to Live Below Your Means

One of the biggest factors of financial freedom and being able to maintain it is you can make your bills and comfortably live throughout the month. In order to do this, you need to make sure that the money coming into your home is more than the money going out. In other words, you want to live below your means.

This is often difficult for a lot of people because they want to have what other people have. They want to have the newer vehicles, the bigger boat, the newest grill, or anything else. People like to have what their friends and neighbors have. However, one factor people don't think about is that their friends and neighbors probably don't have financial freedom. Therefore, you want to take a moment to think about what is more important for you. Would you rather be in debt like your friends or you would rather have financial freedom?

5. Speak with a Financial Advisor

Sometimes the best steps we can take when we are working towards financial freedom is to talk with a financial advisor. They can often give up information and help us with a budget, ways to make sure that we get the most out of our income, and also tell us where we might be spending more money than we should. Furthermore, they can help you figure out what the best investments are, which are always helpful when you are looking at financial freedom. At the same time, they can help you plan for your retirement, which is one of the biggest ways you will be able to remain financially free.

6. Completely Pay Off Your Credit Cards

If you are high-interest credit cards, which is often the case, you want to make sure that you pay these off every month. Therefore, your credit card spending should become part of your budget. What this means is you don't want to use your credit card for whatever you feel like. Instead, you want to create a list of when you can and when you can't use your credit card. For example, you might agree that it is fine in emergency situations or during Christmas shopping. You might also feel that you can use it during tips because it has trip insurance attached to it. Whatever you decide, you want to make sure you follow.

You also want to make sure that you pay off any high-interest loans. When it comes to loans that are lower in interest, they won't affect you too much.

7. Track Your Spending

Along with making sure you follow your budget; you also want to track your spending. There are several reasons for this. First, it will help you make sure that your budget is on track. We often forget about automatic bills that are paid monthly or don't realize how much we really spend every month. These factors can make our budget off, which can cause an obstacle when you are working to reaching and keeping your financial freedom.

Fortunately, there are numerous apps available for download, many of which are free, that will help you to quickly track your spending. Some of these apps include Mint or Personal Capital. These apps typically give you all the information you need and will automatically tell you how much you are spending and how much income you still hold at the end of the month. Most of these apps will also give you charts to help you see your spending habits in a different way.

8. Make Sure to Keep Your Mindset

This is a mindset that you will want to continue to have while you are living financially free. With this mindset, you will not only feel grateful for where you are in life, but you will also remember where you once were. This will help you work towards protecting your financial freedom instead of falling back into credit card debt.

Of course, you can adjust your mindset the way you want to once you reach financial freedom. However, you will want to make sure that you keep your mindset positive. After all, a positive mindset makes you believe that you can accomplish anything.

Chapter 19.   Template Examples and Simulations

Template 1

This is the primary format that we will invest some energy in. It will incorporate the entirety of the various parts that you need to get the message to the correct gatherings, and it is quite basic. Recollect that this is only a layout, and we can go through and utilize this as a guide or a blueprint. On the off chance that it doesn't by and large coordinate with what you need, you can roll out certain improvements, or you can decide to utilize one of the different layouts that we will have access to.

Name

Address

Telephone Number

Record # (make a point to incorporate this on the off chance that you have that data).

Name of the Company Contacting/Point of Contact Person

Important Department

Address

Date

Dear [Include the name of the credit revealing office or utilize the name of the contact party in the event that you approach this information]

I'm composing today to practice my entitlement to scrutinize the legitimacy of the obligation your office claims I owe, compliant with the FCRA, Fair Credit Reporting Act.

As expressed in Section 609 of the FCRA, (2) €:

"A customer revealing office isn't needed to eliminate precise harsh data from a purchaser's record except if the data is obsolete under Section 609 or can't be checked."

Just like my right, I am mentioning confirmation of the accompanying things:

[This is the place where we will list any of the things that we are hoping to debate, including the entirety of the record names and numbers that have been recorded with your credit report]

Furthermore, I have featured these things on the joined duplicate of the credit report I got.

I demand that all future correspondence be done through the mail or email. As expressed in the FCRA, you are needed to react to my debate within 30 days of receipt of this letter. In the event that you neglect to offer a reaction, all contested data should be erased.

Much obliged to you for your brief regard for this matter.

Earnestly,

[Add your mark to this part]

[Print your name here]

See appended; [This is the place where you will rattle off the entirety of the archives that you will connect with this letter]

*Make sure that you join duplicates of your verification of personality, including your introduction to the world date, name, SSN, and your present street number. You additionally need to join a duplicate of your credit report, ensuring that you featured the entirety of the significant things to make it simpler for the invested individuals to perceive what you are discussing.

Template 2

There are a ton of times when the primary format that we talked about will be sufficient for your necessities and can assist you with completing the entirety of the work. Then again, it could be conceivable that you need to discuss the debate in an alternate way, or you just didn't care for the arrangement or something different about the other layout that we went through. That is okay. The accompanying layout will be the one that we can work with too. It discusses a ton of the very issues that we did above however will have a couple of different parts added to it to make this work too. The third format that we can work with incorporates:

Name

Address

Telephone Number

Record # (make a point to incorporate this in the event that you have that data).

Name of the Company Contacting/Point of Contact Person

Important Department

Address

Date

Dear Sir or Madam

I'm writing to practice my entitlement to debate the accompanying things on my document. I have caused a note of these things on the joined duplicate of the report I to have gotten from your organization. You will likewise discover connected duplicates of reports that help to show my personality, SSN, birthdate, and current location.

As expressed in the FCRA, or Fair Credit Reporting Act, Section 609:

[This will be the segment where we incorporate a couple of pertinent statements that depend on what space of Section 609 you might want to debate at that point. You can return to the past section to perceive what a portion of these statements is about, or you can go to the FTC's site to get the authority report that has the specific verbiage that you need. Recollect that you need to note which of the sub-segments you are citing from as well].

The things that I wish to question are as per the following:

- 1. [This is the part where you will incorporate however many significant things as you can. You can have up to 20, yet attempt to just work with the ones that bode well for you].
- 2. [Keep as a main priority that the subtleties will be the most significant with this one. You need to incorporate the name and the quantity of the record, as recorded on your credit report]

These are [inaccurate, wrong, unverified] because of the absence of approval by various gatherings that is needed by Section 609. I have appended duplicates of important documentation.

I would see the value in your help with researching this way inside the following 30 days. As needed by the FCRA, on the off chance that you neglect to do as such, all previously mentioned data/questioned things should be erased from the report.

Genuinely:

[Add your mark to this part]

[Print your name here]

See connected; [This is the place where you will drill down the entirety of the records that you will append with this letter]

*Make sure that you append duplicates of your verification of personality, including your introduction to the world date, name, SSN, and your present postage information. You likewise need to connect a duplicate of your credit report, ensuring that you featured the entirety of the significant things to make it simpler for the invested individuals to perceive what you are discussing.

Template 3

We have investigated some truly genuine instances of the format that you can use with regards to working with Section 609 and ensuring that you can get the credit offices to delete a portion of the awful stuff that is on your reports and causing you a ton of issues en route. In any case, we will investigate a fourth layout that we can use also.

You will see that this one will be really like what we have done in the last two, yet there are some various approaches to introduce the data and various words that are being utilized also. We should investigate this model and perceive how it very well may be comparable or not the same as the other two layouts that we are working with:

Name

Address

Telephone Number

Record # (make a point to incorporate this in the event that you have that data).

Name of the Company Contacting/Point of Contact Person

Applicable Department

Address

Date

To the responsible party in question,

This letter is a proper debate as per the Fair Credit Reporting Act (FCRA).

Endless supply of my credit report, I have discovered that there are a few off base and unconfirmed things. These have adversely affected my present capacity to get credit, and have given pointless shame and bother.

As I am certain you know, it is my right, as indicated by Section 609 of the FCRA, to demand a legitimate examination concerning these errors. Specifically, I am referring to Section 609 (c) (B) (iii), which records "the privilege of a purchaser to question data in the document of the buyer" under the "model synopsis of the privileges of shoppers."

All things considered, coming up next are things I wish to question on my credit report:

1. [This is the part where you will incorporate however many applicable things as you have. You can do up to 20. Ensure that you incorporate the name and the number that is recorded on each record on this report.]

I have additionally featured the entirety of the things that are pertinent to the appended duplicate of the said credit report.

As expressed in the FCRA, you are needed to react to my debate within 30 days of receipt of this letter. In the event that you neglect to offer a reaction, all contested data should be erased. I have connected all the significant documentation for your audit. I thank you ahead of time for your brief reaction and goal of this issue.

Truly

[Add your mark to this part]

[Print your name here]

See joined; [This is the place where you will drill down the entirety

*Make sure that you connect duplicates of your evidence of character, including your introduction to the world date, name, SSN, and your present street number. You additionally need to connect a duplicate of your credit report, ensuring that you featured the entirety of

the applicable things to make it simpler for the invested individuals to perceive what you are discussing.

Template 4

This will be a somewhat unique sort of letter than what we saw previously. This will be significant in light of the fact that it assists us with following up on the off chance that we have not heard a single thing from the other party. Recall that we are allowing them 30 days to go through and give us a reaction or the like, or they naturally need to take that off their reports. The 30 days starts when they get the letter you send, not when you compose it or when you send it. This is another motivation behind why it is critical to go through and get it sent through confirmed mail, so you have a precise date close by.

At the point when the 30 days are finished, the time has come to do a subsequent letter. This will be the point at which you let the organization realize that the 30 days are finished and that you anticipate that things on your report should be deleted and finished as quickly as time permits. That is the reason we will work with the accompanying to assist us with composing the subsequent letter that we need.

Name

Address

Telephone Number

Record # (make a point to incorporate this in the event that you have that data).

Name of the Company Contacting/Point of Contact Person

Important Department

Address

Date

Dear Sir or Madam

My name is [Your name], and I contacted you a little while back in regards surprisingly report. This letter is to inform you that you have not reacted to my underlying letter, dated [insert date]. I have repeated the provisions of my question beneath for your benefit.

[This is the place where we will embed data from the letter we expounded initially on the contested things. Incorporate questioned account names and numbers as recorded on your credit report.]

Area 609 of the FCRA states that you should explore my debate inside 30 schedule days from my underlying letter. As you have neglected to do as such, I generously demand that you eliminate the previously mentioned things from my credit report.

Any further remarks or questions can be coordinated to my lawful delegate, [insert name], and I can be reached at [insert telephone number].

Genuinely

[Add your mark to this part]

[Print your name here]

See joined; [This is the place where you will rattle off the entirety of the reports that you will connect with this letter]

*Make sure that you connect duplicates of your evidence of character, including your introduction to the world date, name, SSN, and your present street number. You additionally need to append a duplicate of your credit report, ensuring that you featured the entirety of the pertinent things to make it simpler for the invested individuals to perceive what you are discussing

Conclusion

Your credit report is the most important report you have. It can prevent you from obtaining a mortgage, car loan, or another type of financing for a new home or car purchase. You should take steps to protect your credit and check your credit report on an annual basis to look for any inaccuracies that may be affecting your score.

As you become older, having a strong credit history can make things easier for you since lenders will be more inclined to give money to someone who has a track record of managing their finances responsibly and not missing payments or incurring late fees. If not handled properly, mistakes in your past could haunt you for years to come.

Taking a proactive approach to your credit will help you rectify any inaccuracies that are discovered and take the necessary steps to maintain a positive credit history. If you want to make a change in the way your credit score is calculated and influence what information is reported, you must fill out and submit the proper forms to the major credit-rating agencies (Equifax, Experian, and Trans Union) that track your financial activity. These forms are called "opt-ins" or "opt-outs" and can be obtained from each of the three major credit bureaus. Apply for an extended fraud alert or a security freeze on your account if you detect anything improper with your credit report.

When you move, it can be difficult to have information in your credit report updated by your creditors. This is because you have little control over the information they provide about your payments. In effect, the new notice of address change that you send them will be ignored. The best way to ensure that your information is correct is to initiate a "credit freeze." This prevents all lenders from seeing or changing your credit report without first getting permission from you. A credit freeze does not prevent the lenders from opening an account for you or extending credit from them, but ensures that no changes are made without your approval.

www.ingramcontent.com/pod-product-compliance
Lightning Source LLC
Chambersburg PA
CBHW081427220526
45466CB00008B/2296